W9-BAL-353

california
ARCHAEOLOGY
VOLUME 4 : ISSUE 2 : DECEMBER 2012

ARTICLES

REPORT

REVIEWS

NEWS AND NOTES   *Compiled by Shelly Davis-King*

Erratum for Volume 4, Issue 1, Page 103, figure 3 caption should indicate that existing salt streams are solid beaded lines rather than solid black lines.

Cover: Coso rock art panel at CA-INY-43 in Parrish Gorge, northern Coso Range showing bighorn sheep ram skull atop a pole. See figure 6 (courtesy of Don Austin) in article by Yohe and Garfinkel.

ISBN: 978–1–61132–805–9

california

ARCHAEOLOGY
VOLUME 4 : ISSUE 2 : DECEMBER 2012

TERRY L. JONES, *Editor*
  Department of Social Sciences, California Polytechnic State University, San Luis Obispo, CA

JILL K. GARDNER, *Managing Editor*
  Jill K. Gardner & Associates, Inc., 1199 Pacific Highway, Unit 703, San Diego CA 92101

KENT LIGHTFOOT, *Associate Editor, Historical Archaeology*
  Department of Anthropology, 232 Kroeber Hall, University of California, Berkeley, CA

DON LAYLANDER, *Associate Editor, Baja California*
  ASM Affiliates, Inc., 2034 Corte Del Nogal, Carlsbad, CA

KATHLEEN HULL, *Reviews Editor*
  Department of Anthropology, University of California, Merced, CA

SHELLY DAVIS-KING, *News and Notes Editor*
  Davis-King & Associates, P. O. Box 10, Standard, CA

Obsidian Sources of Northern Baja California

The Known and the Unknown

Lee M. Panich

Department of Anthropology, Santa Clara University, 500 El Camino Real, Santa Clara, CA 95053 (lpanich@scu.edu)

Antonio Porcayo Michelini

Centro INAH, Baja California, Reforma No. 1333, Col. Nueva 2a. Sección, Mexicali, Baja California, CP 21100 (antonio_porcayo@yahoo.com.mx)

M. Steven Shackley

Department of Anthropology, University of California, Berkeley, 232 Kroeber Hall, Berkeley, CA 94720 (shackley@berkeley.edu)

Abstract   The obsidian sources of northern Baja California remain under-studied even though archaeological work in the region has expanded in recent decades. In this article, we provide descriptions and geochemical characterizations for several known and as-yet unlocated sources of artifact quality obsidian in the northern region of Baja California. These data include two new sources recorded in the field, one additional unknown source identified in an archaeological assemblage, and one unknown source found only in secondary geological deposits. We also address the distribution of obsidian in secondary geological contexts. This article should serve as the basis for future provenance work as well as to further our understanding of indigenous trade networks and procurement strategies.

Resumen   Los yacimientos de obsidiana del norte de Baja California siguen siendo desconocidos aunque el trabajo arqueológico en la región se ha ido incrementado en décadas recientes. En este artículo proporcionamos descripciones y caracterizaciones geoquímicas para varios yacimientos de obsidiana, conocidos y desconocidos, de artefactos de la región norte de Baja California. Estos datos incluyen dos nuevos yacimientos registrados en campo, un yacimiento desconocido identificado en una colección arqueológica, así como un yacimiento desconocido adicionale identificado solamente en contextos secundarios geológicos. También discutimos la distribución de obsidiana geológica en contextos secundarios. Este

California Archaeology, Volume 4, Number 2, December 2012, pp. 183–200.

artículo debe servir como base para futuros trabajos de identificación de procedencia así como para de manera adicional incrementar nuestra comprensión de las redes de intercambio y estrategias de adquisición indígenas.

The geological sources and archaeological distribution of obsidian in northern Baja California remain relatively unknown, even as obsidian provenance studies have proliferated in other parts of western North America. This situation is unfortunate since a growing number of Mexican and American archaeologists are conducting research in the region and obsidian from Baja California sources is occasionally found in sites in southern California. The area around the modern city of San Felipe has long been thought to be the geological source region of most obsidian artifacts found in archaeological contexts in the central and northern portions of the state of Baja California. Recent research, however, complicates this picture. New sources have been identified in the field, well to the north and south of San Felipe, and laboratory analysis of archaeological specimens and samples from secondary geological deposits has identified multiple chemical groups whose primary source localities remain unknown. In this article, we take stock of the state of knowledge regarding obsidian sources in the northern region of Baja California, ranging from the latitude of El Rosario to the international border (Figure 1).

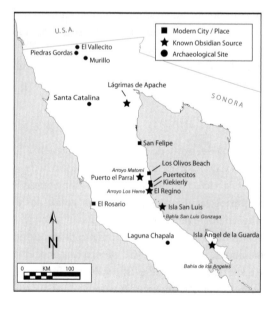

Figure 1. Map of northern Baja California showing locations discussed in text.

The data presented here are from an ongoing binational research project, organized by the authors, that is designed to further our understanding of obsidian sources, distribution, and use in Baja California. The project database includes archaeological and geological samples collected by Antonio Porcayo as part of the Salvamento Arqueológico San Felipe-Laguna Chapala and the Proyecto Registro y Rescate de Sitios Arqueológicos de Baja California–Fase Municipio de Mexicali in 2009 and 2010, as well as archaeological samples collected by one of us (Panich) during research at the site of Mission Santa Catalina from 2005 to 2007. Two of us (Porcayo and Panich) collected additional geological samples in 2011. The third author (Shackley) performed trace element analysis using a Thermo Scientific *Quant'X* energy dispersive x-ray fluorescence (XRF) spectrometer at the Archaeological XRF Laboratory in Berkeley, California. Shackley also provided original data for the San Felipe and Puerto el Parral sources discussed below. Our preliminary findings include the identification of two new geological sources in the field, as well as the presence of multiple, as-yet unlocated sources of obsidian in the region.

History of Research

The history of research into the obsidian sources of northern Baja California is long but intermittent. In 1971, Tom Banks published a short note on the geological sources of obsidian in Baja California and southern California, at which time only two were known. In addition to Obsidian Butte in Imperial County in Alta California, he noted a source in Baja California that was "50 miles south of San Felipe . . . at an elevation [of] 2500 feet in rough volcanic mountains" (Banks 1971:25). While Banks did not reveal the exact location of the source, the distance of the source from San Felipe places it to the south of Arroyo Matomí, which itself has attracted significant attention as a probable source of Baja California obsidian. For instance, both Bouey (1984:55–56) and Hughes (1986) referred to Arroyo Matomí as an obsidian source. However, in his observations of obsidian flakes in archaeological sites at a palm oasis at the upper end of the arroyo, Douglas (1981:68) suggested that the geological source of the obsidian was located somewhere to the south rather than in Arroyo Matomí itself.

In 1984, Bouey (1984:55) provided a qualitative XRF analysis of obsidian samples collected from a drainage described as being south of San Felipe and north of Arroyo Matomí. Although this work represented the first relatively systematic attempt to chemically characterize Baja California obsidian with XRF, and established the term "San Felipe" for this source of obsidian, the data are not directly comparable to quantitative data used today. Nevertheless, Bouey's work strongly suggested that San Felipe obsidian was distinct from that found in the Arroyo

Matomí drainage (Bouey 1984:55). The samples used today to quantitatively as-
sign obsidian artifacts to the San Felipe source were collected in the 1960s by Steven Shackley, who obtained the small nodules from secondary geological deposits
south of San Felipe (Table 1). As with the nodules analyzed by Bouey, information
regarding the exact location where Shackley's San Felipe source nodules were collected has subsequently been lost.

In the 1990s, geological research in the Puertecitos Volcanic Province, near
the modern village of Puertecitos approximately 75 kilometers (km) south of San
Felipe, shed new light on the geological structure of the region (Martín-Barajas et
al. 1995; Nagy et al. 1999; Stock et al. 1999) and on the distribution of artifact-
quality obsidian. At that time, geologist Joann Stock sent Shackley a number of
mapped samples from three localities on a dome complex near Puerto el Parral
rancho just south of Arroyo Matomí.

With the discovery of the Puerto el Parral source, however, the composition
of what constitutes the "San Felipe" and "Arroyo Matomí" obsidians became complicated. Shackley's elemental analysis of samples from Puerto el Parral and the
nodules he collected from the secondary geological deposits south of San Felipe
supported Bouey's (1984) initial observation that there were at least two chemical groups in the Puertecitos Volcanic Province, although the only eruptive event
that was known at the time was that of Puerto el Parral. Given the intermittent
attention paid to Baja California obsidian studies, the relationship between the
newly discovered Puerto el Parral source and the obsidian called "Arroyo Matomí"
by some previous researchers (e.g., Hughes 1986:43) had not been fully explored.
Moreover, the relationship of Puerto el Parral to the source described by Banks
(1971) is not clear, as the distance from San Felipe to Puerto el Parral does not
match Banks' description. We attempt to address some of these lingering questions below.

Further south, the regions around Bahía San Luis Gonzaga and Bahía de los
Angeles also contain multiple obsidian chemical groups observed in geological
contexts and in archaeological assemblages. At least two islands in the Gulf of
California contain obsidian. The volcanic Isla San Luis is known to have extensive
geological obsidian deposits (Paz Moreno and Demant 1999), but the archaeological use of this obsidian has not been documented. The characterization of Isla
San Luis obsidian provided here is from geological contexts only (Table 1). Com-
paratively large quantities of obsidian from the nearby Isla Angel de la Guarda
have also been noted in peninsular archaeological contexts investigated by Ritter
(1994, 1995, 1997). Although the island has long been known to have geological
deposits of obsidian, the nature of the obsidian quality, availability, and exploitation on Isla Angel de la Guarda (as elsewhere in northern Baja California) remains

Table 1. Geological Samples of Artifact Quality Obsidian, Northern Baja California.

Geological Source	Mn	Fe	Rb	Sr	Y	Zr	Nb
Lágrimas de Apache	242	9542	121	59	43	137	6
Lágrimas de Apache	277	9831	116	56	42	130	7
"San Felipe"	320	13643	124	43	36	160	12
"San Felipe"	285	11041	107	35	32	139	4
"San Felipe"	272	10876	143	64	32	176	13
"San Felipe"	263	10221	105	38	33	148	7
"San Felipe"	265	9939	104	37	32	138	12
"San Felipe"	273	10693	104	40	35	146	6
"San Felipe"	256	10006	104	37	32	139	7
"San Felipe"	273	9965	100	39	30	137	10
Puerto el Parral	311	13021	138	60	33	215	17
Puerto el Parral	292	12751	140	64	36	214	16
Puerto el Parral	368	17532	164	72	39	243	19
Puerto el Parral	279	11179	126	60	35	209	13
Puerto el Parral	343	14977	151	69	37	230	14
Puerto el Parral	328	13251	141	65	34	229	13
Puerto el Parral	300	12190	121	57	33	198	14
Puerto el Parral	294	12045	133	60	34	213	12
Puerto el Parral	270	10663	120	59	33	205	13
Puerto el Parral	307	13481	134	60	34	217	14
Kiekierly	246	12138	172	54	34	193	7
Kiekierly	257	12124	165	57	35	189	10
El Regino	237	13465	154	65	40	250	11
El Regino	213	15011	158	65	40	247	3
El Regino	177	12678	148	60	36	235	11
El Regino	195	12708	155	59	35	234	7
El Regino	251	14455	164	60	43	244	5
El Regino	231	13929	197	62	40	242	7
Isla San Luis	603	24268	67	181	36	357	3
Isla San Luis	493	23075	64	195	37	311	6

Note: Values from San Felipe and Puerto el Parral are from Shackley's original source material; all others are from samples collected by Porcayo and Panich as part of this project.

to be definitively settled (Anderson 1950; Bowen 2009a; Ritter 2006:174). Bowen (2009b:67, 2012) has conducted extensive archaeological surveys on the island and has reported multiple primary obsidian source localities of both low and high quality, as well as sites characterized as "obsidian quarry-workshops."

In addition to the obsidian from Isla Angel de la Guarda, Ritter's work at peninsular sites near Bahía de los Angeles has also yielded several artifacts and nodules whose chemistry does not match any known sources in the region (Ritter 1994, 1995, 1997). These include chemical groups reported as Unknowns A, B, C, D, and E, as well as one obsidian chemical group that has been dubbed Ensenada el Pescador. These chemical groups, and the island deposits, are mentioned here simply to convey the complexity of the situation and are not discussed further in this article.

Recent Obsidian Provenance Research in Baja California

The data presented here are part of our ongoing research into the sources and distribution of archaeological obsidian in the state of Baja California, and include obsidian artifacts from 20 archaeological sites as well as more than 40 samples from primary and secondary geological contexts. While the cultural implications of the distribution of archaeological obsidian analyzed as part of this study will not be discussed at length in this article, we nonetheless hope to provide a first step toward a more comprehensive understanding of indigenous trade and procurement strategies in northern Baja California by taking stock of what we know—and do not know—about the geological availability of obsidian in the region. We divide our comments between obsidian chemical groups whose primary source locality is known and those for which the primary source locality is unknown. The list of known sources includes Puerto el Parral and two primary source localities discovered by Antonio Porcayo during his research in northeastern Baja California, Lágrimas de Apache and El Regino.

The Known Sources

Puerto el Parral. As discussed above, the Puerto el Parral source was the first geological source in the region to be definitively located and characterized using comparable quantitative methods. It lies directly south of Arroyo Matomí northwest of Puertecitos in the northern extent of the Sierra Santa Isabel. The source exhibits abundant nodules embedded in perlitic lava. The archaeological distribution of Puerto el Parral glass extends to the Pacific Coast in the San Quintín-El Rosario region, where Moore (2001) reported that it was recovered from multiple sites from varying temporal contexts. Given its proximity to Arroyo Matomí, we suspect that Puerto el Parral is the same obsidian previously referred to by some researchers as "Arroyo Matomí." It should be noted, however, that other researchers have used the terms Arroyo Matomí and San Felipe synonymously (Panich et al. 2010). Future researchers will thus need to compare the original elemental data for obsidian artifacts to the growing list of geological sources in the region to determine the accuracy of previous source assignments.

Lágrimas de Apache. Lágrimas de Apache (ASU 12-1), Spanish for Apache tears, was first recorded in 2008 (Porcayo Michelini and Rojas Chávez 2009). Located near the mouth of the Colorado River, it is the northernmost known geological source of obsidian in Baja California (Figure 1). The obsidian is found in masses of perlite at the mid-elevations of a volcanic dome covered in rhyolitic boulders and rocks. Possible extraction areas have been noted in three places on the dome; in each area, the surface rocks have been removed to expose the perlite lenses beneath. The perlite contains small, rounded to subangular obsidian marekanites, or unmodified obsidian nodules, measuring two to five centimeters (cm). The samples analyzed here were obtained directly from the perlite lenses. No debitage or other cultural materials have been noted at the extraction areas (Porcayo Michelini et al. 2011). Thus far, only one artifact analyzed as part of this project—a flaked nodule collected from a site near El Mayor—can be assigned to the Lágrimas de Apache source, suggesting that its use as toolstone may have been limited.

El Regino. El Regino is a broadly distributed obsidian chemical group, named for a primary source locality near a small prehistoric rockshelter approximately 10 km south of Puertecitos. The geological obsidian deposits were discovered during archaeological reconnaissance for the San Felipe-Laguna Chapala Highway Project (Porcayo Michelini 2011), and the primary source locality at El Regino is an area of volcanic tuff that includes small, rounded to subangular obsidian marekanites up to five cm in diameter. The source is near Arroyo Los Heme and is less than five km north of Volcán Prieto. The samples analyzed as part of this project were collected from the surface and from secondary deposits associated with road construction at the El Regino site. Preliminary survey suggests that obsidian nodules with similar chemistry are present in Arroyo Los Heme as well as beaches associated with Arroyo el Huerfanito some 15 km south of El Regino (Panich and Porcayo Michelini 2012).[1] The geographic extent of the obsidian chemical group noted at El Regino and surrounding areas is a subject of continuing research.

As with Lágrimas de Apache, El Regino obsidian has not been noted in many archaeological assemblages, although sample size may be an issue, as only a small quantity of archaeological obsidian from northeastern Baja California has been analyzed with knowledge of the new chemical groups reported here. A small rock-shelter with prehistoric archaeological deposits is located directly on top of the obsidian-bearing strata at El Regino (Porcayo Michelini et al. 2011), and while no worked obsidian was recovered from the archaeological excavations, multiple small nodules were present in the cultural strata. All of the nodules recovered archaeologically from the El Regino rockshelter, including several red obsidian nodules, are part of the broader El Regino chemical group. One flake of El Regino obsidian was identified at Caro's Cave, another small prehistoric rockshelter, located approximately 3.5 km south of the southernmost extent of the El Regino obsidian nodules in secondary geological contexts.

The Unknown Sources

San Felipe. The obsidian referred to as San Felipe glass is perhaps the best known of the unknown sources in Baja California. San Felipe obsidian has previously been reported in archaeological contexts as far north as Riverside and San Diego counties and as far west as the Pacific Coast (Laylander 2006; McFarland 2000; Moore 2001), making it the most widely distributed source in northern Baja California. Yet its exact geological source is unknown, and its geochemical signature—which includes one nodule that may be from a separate chemical group (Figure 2, Table 1)—is derived from samples collected from secondary geological deposits of only vague provenance. Although the terms San Felipe and Arroyo Matomí have occasionally been used synonymously, Bouey's (1984:55) description of secondary obsidian-bearing deposits north of Arroyo Matomí has long suggested that the San Felipe source is not located in Arroyo Matomí.

Our research supports the notion that the geological source of San Felipe obsidian is well north of Arroyo Matomí. During fieldwork in 2011, we collected several unmodified nodules from Los Olivos, a beach where Arroyo Matomí empties into the Gulf of California. None of the samples from this area of the Arroyo Matomí outwash cluster with the primary group of samples from the San Felipe source (Figure 3). We also noted the presence of unmodified obsidian nodules at a beach approximately 35 km south-southeast of San Felipe. These nodules have not yet been analyzed with comparable methods, but preliminary data using a portable XRF instrument suggest that the nodules are from the San Felipe chemical group. Moreover, the beach is within the general area where the nodules analyzed by Shackley and Bouey were collected decades ago. These two patterns support Bouey's (1984:55) observation that San Felipe obsidian is not present in Arroyo Matomí. The primary source locality for San Felipe obsidian, however, remains unknown.

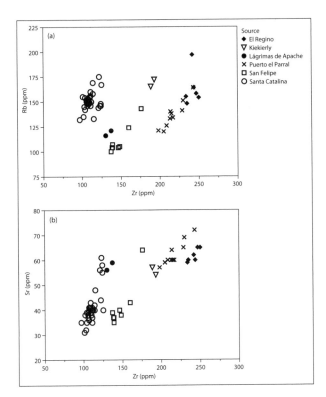

Figure 2. Biplots discriminating obsidian sources in northern Baja California: Rb versus Zr (top) and Sr versus Zr (bottom).

Others. As part of our research, we have identified two other obsidian chemical groups whose primary source localities are currently unknown. One group, similar in chemical composition to San Felipe glass, has to date only been found in archaeological contexts. This chemical group was first noted at the Dominican mission site of Santa Catalina in the southern Sierra Juárez, where a number of obsidian artifacts were recovered from surface collection and excavation (Panich 2011). None of the artifacts from Mission Santa Catalina can be assigned to the existing list of obsidian sources in the region (including possible sources in Alta California and western Arizona), and while some variation exists, they appear to all derive from a single source or source area (Figure 2, Table 2). Interestingly, three obsidian artifacts from different archaeological sites in the northern Sierra Juárez also appear to belong to this chemical group. These include two obsidian flakes collected by INAH archaeologist Julia Bendímez Patterson from the sites of Piedras Gordas and Murillo, as well as one obsidian flake collected by Porcayo from Abrigo del Metate in El Vallecito (Panich et al. 2010, 2011).

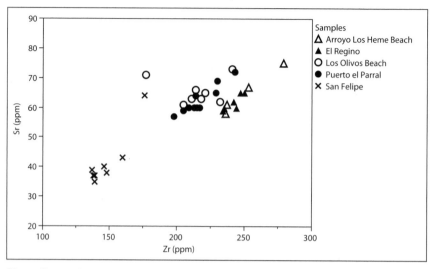

Figure 3. Detail of Sr versus Zr biplot for samples from Los Olivos (Arroyo Matomí) and Arroyo Los Heme beaches compared to sources discussed in text (vitrophyric nodules from beach contexts excluded to preserve scale).

An additional chemical group that suggests an unknown geological obsidian source derives from two unmodified nodules collected from an arroyo during the survey of a plot of land dubbed Kiekierly, located on the Gulf of California coast approximately five km south of Puertecitos on the eastern slope of the Sierra Santa Isabel. These nodules also exhibit elemental concentrations that failed to match the existing chemical signatures of obsidian sources in the region (Figure 2, Table 2). Although only two unmodified nodules are included in the data presented here, subsequent visits to the area have documented the presence of numerous obsidian nodules in the arroyo outwash and beach, suggesting a primary source locality further inland in the arroyo system. Interestingly, an obsidian nodule collected by Porcayo from an archaeological site in the Laguna Chapala region clusters with the Kiekierly obsidian.

Secondary Geological Deposits

Complicating our understanding of the three unknown sources discussed above, as well as the cultural implications of indigenous obsidian procurement, is the fact that many of the obsidian sources in Baja California are found in secondary geological deposits in the dunes and beaches of the Gulf of California coast, as well as in the arroyos of the eastern slopes of the region's mountain ranges. Although

Table 2. Archaeological Specimens from Mission Santa Catalina Indicating Unknown Source or Source Area.

Cat. No.	Mn	Fe	Rb	Sr	Y	Zr	Nb	Comments
PP-6	279	10891	146	61	34	123	7	angular shatter
PP-18	279	8910	149	39	36	109	0	angular shatter
PP-21	248	8701	142	39	33	104	12	angular shatter; red
PP-28	287	9965	169	42	26	114	16	angular shatter
PP-34	252	10319	156	40	39	111	9	angular shatter
PP-35	252	10170	156	37	36	111	5	point fragment
PP-36	263	9962	158	40	37	114	6	flake fragment
PP-37	267	10647	167	40	38	125	8	angular shatter
PP-38	224	9864	151	36	33	107	6	point fragment
PP-39	228	9495	148	40	36	107	10	angular shatter
PP-41	282	11365	148	58	37	124	5	edge-modified flake
PP-43A	235	9854	145	32	28	103	6	point fragment
PP-43B	252	9650	149	40	32	110	5	angular shatter
PP-44	292	12399	175	44	41	122	11	flake fragment
PP-45	259	9505	149	41	35	107	6	angular shatter
PP-50	287	11368	146	55	32	124	5	projectile point
PP-51	222	8955	132	35	34	97	3	flake
PP-52	242	9871	154	38	36	110	7	angular shatter
PP-53	271	11763	144	56	36	121	7	flake fragment
PP-54	242	10111	133	48	30	115	8	angular shatter
PP-55	237	9678	154	35	37	104	3	flake fragment
PP-56	261	10210	160	35	35	111	9	flake fragment
PP-57	260	9600	150	40	36	112	4	angular shatter
PP-58	256	9871	151	39	34	106	10	angular shatter
PP-59A	245	9601	155	38	32	110	11	angular shatter
PP-59B	257	9638	150	37	34	106	6	flake fragment
SCU13-5	262	8799	146	40	32	111	4	flake
SCU16-4	212	8295	135	38	33	102	7	angular shatter
U1S1-13	269	9039	148	43	28	109	4	flake fragment
U20S2-9	266	10356	151	38	35	106	7	angular shatter
U21S2-18A	246	9363	155	31	35	101	9	angular shatter
U22S1-18	282	10651	153	41	33	108	3	point fragment
U22S2-17	248	9670	146	36	31	107	10	flake fragment
U2S2-7	266	9174	146	41	34	111	8	angular shatter
U8S5-14	256	9656	149	41	33	109	2	point fragment

Table 3. Geological Samples from Beach Contexts at Los Olivos (Arroyo Matomí) and Arroyo Los Heme.

Collection Area	Mn	Fe	Rb	Sr	Y	Zr	Nb
Los Olivos Beach	268	12925	151	73	40	241	17
Los Olivos Beach*	402	16197	140	90	56	409	23
Los Olivos Beach	249	12101	127	61	38	205	10
Los Olivos Beach	231	12903	137	66	30	214	14
Los Olivos Beach	224	11552	152	71	34	177	9
Los Olivos Beach	272	12340	133	63	34	218	10
Los Olivos Beach	271	13587	143	65	33	221	12
Los Olivos Beach	259	13555	139	63	33	211	16
Los Olivos Beach	173	13250	236	62	38	232	6
Arroyo Los Heme Beach*	636	30271	95	121	52	451	8
Arroyo Los Heme Beach	270	18181	190	75	51	279	7
Arroyo Los Heme Beach	211	15255	166	67	44	253	9
Arroyo Los Heme Beach	246	13631	154	58	41	236	7
Arroyo Los Heme Beach	199	12541	148	61	41	237	8

Note: Vitrophyric nodules noted with *.

systematic study of secondary geological deposits of obsidian in Baja California is still in its infancy, and our own analyses are ongoing, we offer the following observations.

First, there appears to be some chemical variation within the secondary geological deposits, at least along the Gulf of California Coast. In 2011, for example, we noted variation among samples of non-artifactual obsidian nodules from two beaches along the Gulf of California Coast within the Puertecitos Volcanic Province. Judgmental samples were collected from Los Olivos, within the main outwash area for Arroyo Matomí approximately 17 km north of Puertecitos. As discussed above, the majority of the analyzed nodules from Los Olivos were assigned to the Puerto el Parral source, which is not surprising considering the proximity of that source to Arroyo Matomí. Nevertheless, the Los Olivos sample also included one nodule that appears to cluster with the El Regino chemical group, as well as one vitrophyric nodule with enriched elemental values (Table 3).[2]

South of Los Olivos, several additional samples were collected from a beach roughly 800 meters east of the El Regino site and at the northern end of the outwash of Arroyo Los Heme. Most of the samples from the beach at Arroyo Los Heme cluster with the samples collected from the nearby El Regino primary source locality (Figure 3), although one vitrophyric nodule exhibited elemental values unlike any other nodules from the immediate area (Table 3). These patterns are particularly interesting, given that the set of nodules used by Shackley to initially characterize San Felipe obsidian also displays some variation (Figure 3).

The importance of the apparent chemical variation of obsidian nodules in these secondary geological contexts lies in the fact that nodules belonging to so many of the obsidian chemical groups discovered thus far are easily available in coastal contexts. In fact, two of the groups discussed here are known only from secondary geological deposits: San Felipe and Kiekierly. The El Regino group also appears to be present in extensive secondary geological deposits. While the current sample of archaeological specimens is too small to draw firm conclusions, we suspect that at least some of the obsidian artifacts created by the region's native peoples were manufactured from nodules collected from secondary geological contexts. Archaeological investigations in the San Felipe area, for example, indicate that indigenous inhabitants regularly used waterworn nodules, presumably from beach contexts, and that the uniform shape of the small nodules may have facilitated bipolar reduction (Porcayo Michelini 2012).

Further research on this topic is clearly needed, but our preliminary work suggests that the relationship between archaeological obsidian artifacts and their geological sources in northern Baja California is not entirely straightforward (and see Shackley [2005:26] for examples from the American Southwest). Three patterns, in particular, should give researchers pause when attempting to understand the cultural implications of the distribution of archaeological obsidian in the region: (1) many of the obsidian chemical groups noted thus far occur in secondary geological contexts; (2) prehistoric people apparently used nodules collected from such contexts, at least in the San Felipe area; and (3) the possibility exists for slight chemical variation among the obsidian nodules found in some secondary geological contexts. Additionally, the long and dynamic history of volcanism in northeastern Baja California (Martín-Barajas et al. 1995; Nagy et al. 1999) necessitates a deeper understanding of the location and timing of the eruptive events that produced the varied obsidian groups found in the region today.

Conclusion

With the addition of the obsidian chemical groups discussed here, there appear to be at least six distinct sources of artifact-quality obsidian located in the northern region of Baja California. The primary source locality is known for two of the sources: Lágrimas de Apache and Puerto el Parral. A third, El Regino, is represented by one small primary source locality that may be part of a broader geological distribution of the same chemical group. The exact locations of the primary source localities for the other three—San Felipe, Kiekierly, and the obsidian recovered at Mission Santa Catalina—remain unknown. Immediately south, in the area around Bahía de los Angeles, there are a number of other obsidian sources, both known and unknown. Our understanding of the chemical groups discussed here is further complicated by the availability of many of them through secondary geological deposits.

While our discussion is limited to the northern extent of the Baja California peninsula, it is clear that the native peoples of the region potentially had access to far more numerous and varied obsidian sources than previously thought. The data and observations provided here are preliminary, and further provenance studies, including detailed survey and mapping of both primary and secondary geological deposits of obsidian (Shackley and Henrickson 2009), will help to clarify the picture of obsidian distribution across the region and by extension allow archaeologists to better understand the dynamics of obsidian procurement and trade in native Baja California.

Acknowledgments

We thank the Instituto Nacional de Antropología e Historia for supporting this project. Érika Moranchel and several students from the Escuela Nacional de Antropología e Historia provided valuable assistance during the field surveys. Thanks also to Professor Joann M. Stock, Geological and Planetary Sciences, California Institute of Technology, for information and samples from the Puerto el Parral source. Professor Stock's expertise in the Puertecitos Volcanic Field has been very helpful for studying the geoarchaeology of the region. We appreciate the generosity of Julia Bendímez Patterson and Eric Ritter for sharing data from their own archaeological research in Baja California. We also thank the three anonymous reviewers from *California Archaeology* for their insightful comments and suggestions.

Notes

1. These nodules were analyzed with a portable XRF instrument and the data obtained are not directly comparable with the other data reported here. Accordingly, we have elected not to include them at this time.

2. In previous presentations of this data (i.e., Panich et al. 2010, 2011), we mistakenly reported the presence of additional obsidian nodules from Los Olivos with highly enriched elemental values. However, subsequent major oxide analysis conducted by Shackley confirmed that these outliers were not obsidian but rather dacite and trachyandesite.

References Cited

Anderson, Charles A.
  1950   *1940 E. W. Scripps Cruise to the Gulf of California, Part I: Geology of Islands and Neighboring Land Areas*. Geological Society of America Memoir No. 43.

Banks, Thomas Jeffrey
  1971   Geologic Obsidian Sources for Baja California. *Pacific Coast Archaeological Society Quarterly* 7(1):24–26.

Bouey, Paul D.
  1984   Obsidian Studies and their Implications for Prehistory. *Pacific Coast Archaeological Society Quarterly* 20(1):55–60.

Bowen, Thomas
  2009a   Archaeology of the Islands of the San Lorenzo Chain, Gulf of California, Mexico. *Proceedings of the Society for California Archaeology* 21:242–248.
  2009b   *The Record of Native Peoples On Gulf of California Islands*. Arizona State Museum Archaeological Series No. 201, Tucson.
  2012   Obsidian Sources on Isla Angel de la Guarda. Paper presented at the 46th Annual Meeting of the Society for California Archaeology, San Diego.

Douglas, Ronald D.
  1981   An Archaeological Reconnaissance in Arriba de Arroyo Matomí, Baja California Norte. *Pacific Coast Archaeological Society Quarterly* 17(1):63–69.

Hughes, Richard E.
  1986   Trace Element Composition of Obsidian Butte, Imperial County, California. *Bulletin of the Southern California Academy of Sciences* 85(1):35–45.

Laylander, Don
  2006   Obsidian Studies and Baja California's Prehistory. *Memorias Balances y Perspectivas 2005: IV Encuentro Binacional–La Antropología e Historia de Baja California* (CD ROM). Centro INAH Baja California, Mexicali.

Martín-Barajas, Arturo, Joann M. Stock, Paul Layer, Brian Hausback, Paul Renne, and Margarita López-Martinez
  1995   Arc-Rift Transition Volcanism in the Puertecitos Volcanic Province, Northeastern Baja California, Mexico. *Geological Society of America Bulletin* 107:407–424.

McFarland, Sharon L.
  2000   Changes in Obsidian Exchange in Southern California. Unpublished Master's thesis, Department of Anthropology, San Diego State University.

Moore, Jerry D.
  2001   Extensive Prehistoric Settlement Systems in Northern Baja California: Archaeological Data and Theoretical Implications from the San Quintín-El Rosario Region. *Pacific Coast Archaeological Society Quarterly* 37(4):30–52.

Nagy, Elizabeth A., Marty Grove, and Joann M. Stock
  1999   Age and Stratigraphic Relationships of Pre- and Syn-Rift Volcanic Deposits in the Northern Puertecitos Volcanic Province, Baja California, Mexico. *Journal of Volcanology and Geothermal Research* 93:1–30.

Panich, Lee M.
  2011   Continuities in a Time of Change: Lithic Technology at Mission Santa Catalina, Baja California. *Pacific Coast Archaeological Society Quarterly* 45(1&2):13–30.

Panich, Lee M., and Antonio Porcayo Michelini
  2012   More Complicated Than We Thought: An Update on the Obsidian Sources of Baja Califor-
          nia. Paper presented at the 46th Annual Meeting of the Society for California Archaeology,
          San Diego.
Panich, Lee M., Antonio Porcayo Michelini, and M. Steven Shackley
  2011   Obsidian Sources of Northern Baja California: The Known and the Unknown. Paper
          presented at the XII Encuentro Binacional: Balances y Perspectivas, Instituto Nacional de
          Antropología e Historia, Mexicali.
Panich, Lee M., Antonio Porcayo Michelini, Julia Bendímez Patterson, and M. Steven Shackley
  2010   Recent Obsidian Provenance Studies in Baja California. Paper presented at the XI Encuen-
          tro Binacional: Balances y Perspectivas, Instituto Nacional de Antropología e Historia,
          Ensenada.
Paz Moreno, Francisco A., and Alain Demant
  1999   The Recent Isla San Luis Volcanic Centre: Petrology of a Rift-Related Volcanic Suite in
          the Northern Gulf of California, Mexico. *Journal of Volcanology and Geothermal Research*
          93:31–52.
Porcayo Michelini, Antonio
  2011   Informe del Salvamento Arqueológico San Felipe–Laguna Chapala Kms 109 + 340 a 117
          + 940 (Excavación), y Propuesta para Siguiente Temporada. Centro INAH Baja California,
          Mexicali.
  2012   Industria Lítica de Puntas de Proyectil Tipo San Felipe. Centro INAH Baja California,
          Mexicali (in press).
Porcayo Michelini, Antonio, and Juan Martín Rojas Chávez
  2009   Informe de la Tercera Temporada de Campo del Proyecto Registro y Rescate de Sitios
          Arqueológicos de Baja California Fase Municipio de Mexicali y Propuesta para la Cuarta
          Temporada de Campo 2009. Centro INAH Baja California, Mexicali.
Porcayo Michelini, Antonio, William Eckhardt, and Juan Martín Rojas Chávez
  2011   Around the 28th to the 32nd Parallel: Prehistoric Quarries of Baja California. Paper pre-
          sented at the 76th Annual Meeting of the Society for American Archaeology, Sacramento.
Ritter, Eric W.
  1994   Informe: Investigaciones de Ecología Social y Cambios entre Culturas Prehistóricas en la
          Región de Bahía de los Ángeles, Baja California (1993). Instituto Nacional de Antropología
          e Historia, Mexico City.
  1995   Informe: Investigaciones de Ecología Social y Cambios entre Culturas Prehistóricas en la
          Región de Bahía de los Ángeles, Baja California (1994). Instituto Nacional de Antropología
          e Historia, Mexico City.
  1997   Informe: Investigaciones de Ecología Social y Cambios entre Culturas Prehistóricas en la
          Región de Bahía de los Ángeles, Baja California (1995). Instituto Nacional de Antropología
          e Historia, Mexico City.
  2006   Bahía de los Angeles. In *The Prehistory of Baja California: Advances in the Archaeology of the
          Forgotten Peninsula*, edited by Don Laylander and Jerry D. Moore, pp. 167–178. University
          Press of Florida, Gainesville.
Shackley, M. Steven
  2005   *Obsidian: Geology and Archaeology in the North American Southwest*. University of Arizona
          Press, Tucson.

Shackley, M. Steven, and Celeste N. Henrickson

    2009   From the Unknown to Known: The State of Obsidian Source Provenance Studies in Baja California. Paper presented at the 74th Annual Meeting of the Society for American Archaeology, Atlanta.

Stock, Joann M., Claudia J. Lewis, and Elizabeth A. Nagy

    1999   The Tuff of San Felipe: An Extensive Middle Miocene Pyroclastic Flow Deposit in Baja California, Mexico. *Journal of Volcanology and Geothermal Research* 93:53–74.

Great Basin Bighorn Ceremonialism

Reflections on a Possible Sheep Shrine at the Rose Spring Site (CA-INY-372), Rose Valley, Alta California

Robert M. Yohe II

Department of Anthropology, California State University, Bakersfield, CA 93311 (Robert_Yohe@firstclass1.csubak.edu)

Alan P. Garfinkel

AECOM, Camarillo, CA 93012-8750 (alan.gold@aecom.com)

Abstract   In the early 1990s, a bighorn ram skull cap with intact horn cores, set atop a stacked rock cairn, was discovered at the Rose Spring site (CA-INY-372), located on the edge of the Coso Range at the southwestern corner of the Great Basin. In this article, we describe the character of the discovery, date the feature, and posit its meaning and function. The feature is intriguing since it might represent a prehistoric manifestation associated with Coso Representational Rock Art. The context for understanding this discovery and other prehistoric bighorn features documented in the Desert West is explored. A review of ethnographic accounts, native oral tradition and cosmology, and bighorn figurative sculptures and rock art, help us explore the religious and ceremonial significance of this animal to the aboriginal people of the region.

Resumen   A principios de los 1990, se descubrieron la parte superior del cráneo de un carnero cimarrón, con los centros de los cuernos intactos, ponida sobre un montículo de piedras en el sitio arqueológico de Rose Spring (CA-INY-372), situado en el borde de la Coso Range, en la esquina suroeste de la Gran Cuenca. En este artículo, describimos el carácter del descubrimiento, datamos el hallazgo, y postulamos su significado y función. El hallazgo es intrigante, ya que pueda representar una manifestación prehistórica asociada con el arte rupestre Coso Representational. Se exploran el contexto para comprender este descubrimiento y otros hallazgos prehistóricos de carnero cimarrón documentados en el Desert West. Una revisión de los informes etnográficos, la tradición oral y cosmología nativa, y el arte de figuras y rupestre del carnero cimarrón, nos ayuda a explorar el significado religioso y ceremonial que tiene este animal a la gente nativa de la región.

California Archaeology, Volume 4, Number 2, December 2012, pp. 201–224.

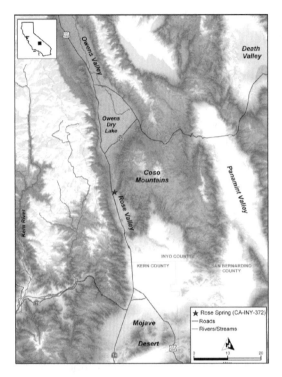

Figure 1. Map showing the location of the Rose Spring site (CA-INY-372) in the eastern Sierra Nevada and western Great Basin.

Bighorn sheep (*Ovis canadensis*) are fascinating animals, both in their physical form and in their behavior. Evidence suggests that these animals were something more than a mere sustenance resource to the aboriginal inhabitants of the Desert West. To explore the religious and ceremonial significance of bighorn sheep, a unique prehistoric archaeological feature is considered. The feature consists of a stacked rock cairn with a bighorn ram partial skull having intact horn cores at its apex. It was discovered at the Rose Spring archaeological site (CA-INY-372) on the western edge of the Coso Range in Rose Valley, east of the Sierra Nevada at the extreme southwestern corner of the Great Basin (Yohe 1992) (Figure 1).

This study describes the character of this discovery, dates the feature, and posits its meaning and function. The feature is all the more intriguing since it perhaps represents a prehistoric manifestation associated with the Coso Representational Rock Art Complex. The contexts for understanding the feature include other bighorn animal bone features documented in the Desert West, the great number of bighorn petroglyphs and effigies in the Great Basin Region, ethnographically documented aboriginal exploitation of bighorn, and the religious traditions of the late prehistoric Numic-speaking peoples of the region.[1]

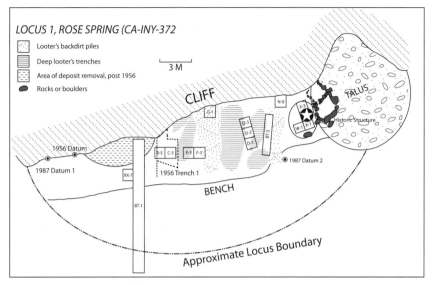

Figure 2. Map of the Rose Spring site (CA-INY-372; Locus 1) showing the general area, the different times of site excavations, and the placement of excavation units and trenches. Excavation unit X-2 is beneath the star that indicates the location of the bighorn sheep feature.

The Rose Spring Bighorn Feature

The bighorn feature discussed here was uncovered during excavations at the Rose Spring site as part of the senior author's dissertation research in 1987 (Yohe 1992, 1997). The partial cranium of the bighorn ram was first revealed at a depth of 80-90 cm below the surface on the western edge of Locus 1 in excavation units X-1 and X-2 (Yohe 1992:49) (Figures 2 and 3). Underlying the horn cores and upper cranium was a rock cairn consisting of a long, plinth-like andesite boulder placed upright into an old hearth and surrounded by fire-cracked stone. The structure of this feature might be better characterized as a stone platform akin to a shrine or altar. Figure 4 provides an artistic reconstruction of what such a feature may have looked like shortly after its construction.

Two radiocarbon dates were obtained from the hearth associated with the bighorn feature. The first was obtained from the top of the hearth, at a depth of 90 cm; the second came from the base of the hearth at 140 cm. The first radiocarbon assay yielded a date of 1,360 ± 70 radiocarbon years before present (RCYBP) and the second produced a date of 1,400 ± 50 RCYBP (Figure 5). When adjusted for their ^{13}C values and calibrated, these ages are equivalent to calendar dates having midpoints of about A.D. 493 and 465, or approximately A.D. 500 (Yohe 1997:49).

Figure 3. Bighorn ram skull and horn core upon exposure during excavation. Pictured in the photograph are Robert Yohe and John Goodman (photograph by Brooke Arkush, 1987).

Figure 4. Artist's reconstruction of the bighorn sheep ram cranium rock feature at the Rose Spring site. Illustration by Michael W. Chittock.

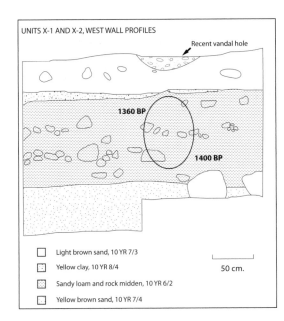

UNITS X-1 AND X-2, WEST WALL PROFILES

Recent vandal hole

1360 BP

1400 BP

Light brown sand, 10 YR 7/3

Yellow clay, 10 YR 8/4

Sandy loam and rock midden, 10 YR 6/2

Yellow brown sand, 10 YR 7/4

50 cm.

Figure 5. Stratigraphic profile of west walls of excavations units X-1 and X-2 and showing the radiocarbon dates. The oval depicts the approximate location of the feature within the stratum. Note the darker stratum that represents the cultural fluorescence during the late Newberry/early Haiwee periods.

A complete and finely executed Humboldt Basal-notched obsidian projectile point was also retrieved from the 80-90 cm level in unit X-1 within a horizontal distance of 50 cm from the bighorn feature. Judging from its completeness and exceptionally fine execution, it appears to have been an offering intended to accompany the feature and was most likely deposited contemporaneously with the use of the feature. The point is a long, slender implement with finely detailed finishing, measuring 70.1 mm in length with a maximum basal width of 24.6 mm, tapering to an average width of 21.6 mm.

Based on its dimensions, and particularly its basal width, this artifact is an example of the Wide subtype of the Humboldt Basal-notched form (Garfinkel and Yohe 2002). This style point, with its distinctive basal morphology and metrics, was most popular during the period from ca. 500 B.C. to A.D. 800. This temporal placement is consistent with the two radiocarbon assays that date the associated feature, and most likely this projectile point, at ca. A.D. 500. Such a date places the cached sheep cranium and rock feature near the Newberry-Haiwee interface, dating to about the terminal Newberry Period (1,200 B.C.-A.D. 600), or perhaps with the initial centuries of the Haiwee Period (A.D. 600-1300). This is a time in eastern California prehistory that is recognized by an unusually frequent pattern of human burials exhibiting grave offerings of multiple projectile points and other associated artifacts (Garfinkel 2007:124-125). Such grave offerings are consistent with the growing importance of status and prestige among the prehistoric inhabitants in the region. Additionally, the Humboldt Basal-notched form has been noted in profusion and is especially correlated with communal game drive and intercept hunting sites that specifically targeted bighorn sheep and pronghorn antelope (Garfinkel and Yohe 2002).

Unfortunately, the condition of the partial bighorn sheep skull was poor and very fragile, in part due to the large and delicate sinuses associated with this portion of the cranium. Both horn cores were present and approximately 10 cm in diameter at the base (maximum dimension) and 19 cm in length (partial measurement). The maximum circumference at the base of the horn core is 25.0 cm. The size of the horn core indicates a mature adult male, probably at least four years old (cf. Hansen and Demming 1980). At the time of excavation, the decision was made not to use a consolidant to help preserve the bone for fear of compromising the accuracy of future attempts at radiocarbon dating. A field photograph of the skull is shown in Figure 3. Attempts to directly radiocarbon date the bighorn sheep bone in 2008 failed due to the lack of any organic fraction in the friable bone (Murray Tamers, personal communication 2008).

This unusual stone accumulation, with an associated artifact and bighorn sheep skull, suggested to us that it might be representative of a feature that functioned outside of the realm of simple subsistence. Complete horn cores of *Ovis canadensis* are virtually nonexistent in the archaeological record of the region. The senior author thought it unusual at the time, but was reticent to conclude that it might have ceremonial implications. As time has passed, and additional data regarding other bighorn features in this region have become available, a reexamination of this anomalous feature suggests that it may indeed have had ritual significance.

Other Bighorn Features in the Far West

The Rose Spring bighorn sheep feature appears to be unique, although a scattering of other prehistoric features containing bighorn sheep bones have been reported in the Far West. Spanish explorers in the seventeenth and eighteenth centuries encountered large accumulations of bighorn sheep horns and deer antlers along the Gila River in the O'odham and Yuman territories of southern Arizona (Castetter and Bell 1942:67; Castetter and Underhill 1935:41). These horn and antler caches reportedly contained thousands of animal skulls. Grant (1980:30) summarized archaeological and ethnohistoric data pertaining to other accumulations of bighorn skulls and horns at sheep kill sites found throughout northwestern Arizona and southwestern Sonora, Mexico (Grant 1980:30). In his diary account from 1774, Juan Bautista de Anza noted that the Papago carried the bighorn sheep horns and stacked them at the Cabeza Prieta Tanks to "control the wind and prevent the air from leaving that place" (Bolton 1930).

In the northern Rocky Mountains region of northwestern Wyoming is Mummy Cave (site 48PA201). This large rockshelter is situated on the banks of the North Fork of the Shoshone River, about 55 km west of Cody. During their excavations at this site, Husted and Edgar (2002:39-40) documented a portion of a bighorn sheep skull possibly associated with a purposeful rock alignment. It was positioned at the base of a slope, adjacent to three vertical stone slabs set in a linear array that created a 1.8-m-long alignment. Husted and Edgar (2002) suggested that the feature may have been a shrine. The feature was dated to about 8,800 RCYBP based on an assay from a nearby fire pit feature.

A bighorn sheep headdress is on exhibit in the Prehistoric Museum at the College of Eastern Utah, in Price, Utah. This artifact was discovered cached in a rock crevice on the eastern edge of the San Rafael Swell, near the Green River in eastern Utah. The headdress was found in two pieces, with drilled holes in the cranium, and a leather headband attached. Six *Olivella* shell beads are scattered around the band but are not attached to it. The sheep horns had been divided in half to minimize their weight and were sewn directly to the skull to ensure permanent attachment. The *Olivella* beads were most likely originally attached to the headdress and the regalia may have been used with the accompanying animal hide hood. Chester King (personal communication 2009) examined some photographs of the *Olivella* sp. shell beads and determined that they are probably of a recognized and chronologically diagnostic type that were drilled and split longitudinally. Such beads typically date to ca. A.D. 1050-1150 (Phase M5c in King's [1990] southern California sequence). Bennyhoff and Hughes (1987:125) referred to these bead types as split-punched forms, which they dated between the Middle/Late Period transition and early Phase I of the Late Period. This was a time when the Fremont expression in the Great Basin was on the wane and it is possible that the headdress might be early Shoshone or Gosiute in affiliation.

About 30 km north of the Reno-Sparks area, in northwestern Nevada, a trophy ram skull was recently discovered at site 26Wa2460 that was identified as a prehistoric village (Young et al. 2009). During excavations at the site, a Middle Archaic house floor was uncovered. In the center of the structure, a bighorn ram skull was discovered. The cached cranium had its horns still attached and appears to have been ritually curated and displayed. Young et al. (2009:249) hypothesized that this cached ram cranium was employed "to reinforce the benefits of a successful hunt . . . [thereby acknowledging] the enhancement of a hunter's prestige within a larger group." The skull was found in association with two complete projectile points, which perhaps served as ritual offerings. Several aboriginal houses at the village site produced radiocarbon ages ranging between 3,700 and 2,800 calibrated RCYBP (cal B.P.), firmly placing the site and the feature itself in a Middle Archaic (4,000-1,500 cal B.P.) context.

At Loyalton Rockshelter in Sierra County, California, in the northern Sierra Nevada, Wilson (1963) excavated a small, temporary hunting camp at 1,800 m above sea level. The site appears to have been a hunting station that was intermittently occupied over thousands of years but was most intensively used during the Middle Archaic. Wilson's (1963) extensive excavations led to the discovery of five individual cache pits containing a total of 12 bighorn sheep skulls from adults (n = 9) and infants (n = 3). Only bighorn sheep cranial elements were interred within these pits. Wilson (1963:63) suggested that these selected bighorn bones indicated their importance as ritual and magical expressions. While only one artifact (a projectile point) was found in direct association with any of the cache pits that contained the sheep skulls, artifacts interpreted as ritual offerings were discovered in other areas of the site, including several bone pins, an exotic obsidian biface, stone pipe bowls, and two ovate charmstones (Wilson 1963).

A bighorn atlas vertebra was uncovered by Sutton and Yohe (1987) during excavations at Nopah Cave, just east of Death Valley in Southern Paiute territory. They argued that this particular skeletal element was interred to physically manifest a Numic myth. In many Numic origin stories, Coyote uses a bighorn atlas vertebra as a penis sheath in order to copulate with a woman who had a deadly toothed vagina that killed her lovers. Coyote successfully reproduces with the girl and the progeny of their union become the various Numic tribes.

In the Tehachapi Mountains of eastern California, just outside the southwestern corner of the Great Basin, is Creation Cave (CA-KER-508), a Kawaiisu (Numic) site within Tomo Kahni State Historic Park. Sutton (2001) reported a burned atlas vertebra of a probable bighorn sheep within this cave dating to the late prehistoric era (ca. A.D. 600 to historic contact). He posited that this skeletal element was related to religious observances associated with Kawaiisu origin traditions (Sutton 2001:21), which indicate that the first people emerged from a bedrock mortar cup in Creation Cave and this was where the Kawaiisu themselves were born (Earle 2000; Harrington 1986; Sutton 1981, 1982; Zigmond 1977:76, 1980:41).

Bighorn Sheep Pictorial Representations

Strong religious associations for bighorn sheep, as a central element of prehistoric Basin cosmology, are suggested by the numerous prehistoric representations of these animals as well as depictions of bighorn hunting scenes. Great Basin rock drawings and paintings of bighorn number in the tens of thousands, and are nowhere more abundant than in the Coso Representational rock art expression recognized in eastern California (Garfinkel 2006, 2007; Grant et al. 1968). In another location, effigies of sheep include more than 1,000 fragmentary split twig figurines discovered at Newberry Cave in the eastern Mojave Desert (Davis and Smith 1981:97-101). The Newberry Cave split twig figurines and the associated men's hunting society activities date to a time centering on 1,500 B.C.

The geographic area of the Rose Spring prehistoric site is the western edge of the Coso Range (Figure 1). During certain periods of prehistory, aboriginal occupants of the Coso Range emphasized large game for the meat portion of their diet and were especially focused on hunting bighorn (Garfinkel 2007; Garfinkel et al. 2009, 2010). Bighorn sheep ceremonialism for the Coso artisans may have had immense symbolic and social importance (e.g., Hildebrandt and McGuire 2002, 2003; McGuire and Hildebrandt 2005). Approximately half of the estimated 100,000 rock art elements that adorn individual basalt boulders and canyon walls are depictions of bighorn. The demonstrated consistency of the Coso bighorn sheep rock art motif, the continuity of these depictions over time, their specialized locations (spatially correlated with hunting blinds, dummy hunters, and game drive sites), and their spatially constrained occurrence within the landscape (located most often in the open on sheer rock faces on the walls of major lava canyons) seem to provide persuasive evidence for placing this conventionalized bighorn sheep ceremonialism at the center of a ritual Coso bighorn sheep cult (Garfinkel 2007; Garfinkel and Austin 2011; Van Tilberg et al. 2011; but see Whitley 1998). Supporting archaeological evidence for a broader, less intensive regional expression of Great Basin bighorn sheep ritualism can be seen in rock art depictions throughout the Desert West (Allen 2011). Such a pattern includes a ritual complex that also incorporated split twig figurines (cf. Coulam and Schroedl 2004) and related religious paraphernalia, such as quartz crystals, paint palettes, and sculpted animal effigies (e.g., Grant 1980).

One notable, but perhaps atypical, example of bighorn ritualism is a Coso rock art drawing of what appears to be a ceremony involving the veneration of a bighorn sheep skull. This drawing, found in Parrish Gorge in the northern Coso Range, is associated with an assemblage of petroglyphs at prehistoric site CA-INY-43 (Grant et al. 1968:39). The panel appears to depict a mountain sheep skull set atop a pole (Figure 6). In the central panel, a large, nearly life-sized (4 feet in height) figure of a man stands with open arms and hands outstretched, seeming to reach for a weighted atlatl. On his back the man appears to be carrying a fringed basket or hide bag and at his feet is a small wand. Additionally, Coso Range rock drawings sometimes depict sheep skulls in a realistic, representational fashion and more commonly the sheep horns are rendered alone and in abstraction with a generalized iconic signature of sheep horns in simplified outline style (Figure 7).

Figure 6. Coso rock art panel in Parrish Gorge showing bighorn sheep ram skull atop a pole. (Drawing courtesy of Don Austin.)

Finally, Miller (1983) postulated that rock art images crafted by prehistoric native peoples in their hunting areas were designed as visual prayers. They were a means of speaking to the spirits, animals, plants, and rocks, to remind them of what the appropriate activities were for the area.

Seasonality and Hunting Techniques for Bighorn Sheep

Bighorn sheep mate in the fall, their rutting season. This is the only time of year when the ranges of rams, ewes, and yearlings coincide (Geist and Petocz 1977; Matheny et al. 1997). During other parts of the year, ewes and rams occupy different habitats. The rutting season is considered one of the best times to hunt bighorn, when they are most vulnerable to predation (Matheny et al. 1997). Moreover, the animals are fattest during the fall as they prepare for a less verdant environment during winter. They are also less wary, because it is a time of considerable tension when rams are intent on breeding.

Figure 7. Rock art panel in Renegade (Little Petroglyph) Canyon, Coso Range, with a frontal view of two bighorn sheep ram skulls with horns and four simplified sheep horn outline glyphs (photograph courtesy of Don Austin).

In the dry deserts of the Great Basin, there were infrequent opportunities for people to come together in larger social gatherings. Fall was one of the most important times for such aggregations, when dispersed aboriginal groups coalesced for communal pronghorn antelope and rabbit drives. This was also the time for seed and nut harvests, during which there were activities associated with feasting, ceremonies, and courting, as well as the Round Dance (or Circle Dance). The Round Dance was held specifically to promote game and to ensure that there would be a bountiful supply of seeds. Hence, the dance was intended "to make seeds grow" and to foster animal and plant fertility (Park 1941:192; Shimkin 1970:177; Steward 1941:323; Stewart 1941; Vander 1997:220).

Gilmore (1953) described a bighorn hunt conducted by the Paiute northeast of Bishop. A Round Dance led by a shaman was held prior to the communal sheep hunt. After the dance and a large feast, the celebrants followed the hunt shaman and/or singer into the local mountains. The hunting party spread out over a large area and worked together to draw the bighorn into a prepared corral. People trapped the sheep by spreading out over the region and gradually closing them in and concentrating them into a narrow chute (a V-shaped wing trap) composed of rocks and brush. This trap led to a corral, where the animals were ultimately slain. The hunt leader, ritualist, or singer stood at the gate and directed where his fellow hunters should shoot.

Alternatively, a solitary hunter could stalk a lone bighorn through the skillful use of a decoy. The hunter used a bighorn skull with horns as a headdress and concealed himself behind rocks and brush. With the horns protruding, he would replicate the sounds of a sheep pawing the ground by plucking his bow. He would then jab and scrape the ground, producing sounds of an aggressive ram preparing for a dominance display. Such activity would attract his quarry, and he could dispatch the beast at close range (typically 25 feet or less) with an arrow directed under the bighorn's chin (Gilmore 1953:150). Julian Steward (1941:220, 423) reported that Great Basin natives thumped logs together or pounded on rocks to attract the curious sheep to the hunters—the bighorn thinking they were hearing rams fighting for breeding rights.

Bighorn Sheep in Numic Traditions and Ceremonies

Steward (1968) believed that animal themes in Great Basin ceremonialism and ritual expression were not major elements of ethnographic Numic religious traditions. However, Malouf (1966:4) asserted that big game hunting rites and group religious ceremonies were strongly imprinted as characteristic elements of Desert West societies.

There may have existed, *in remnant fashion*, a more ancient religious substrate associated with "hunting religions" (Fowler 1986; Hultkrantz 1986a, 1986b). We believe that the religious import of the bighorn sheep and a culture complex of animal ceremonialism existed only in relict fashion among Numic cultures. These earlier elements can be reconstructed from a careful and selective review of certain recurrent patterns expressed in Great Basin oral traditions and rituals.

Whitley (1982) pointed out the potential symbolic significance of bighorn sheep in Great Basin oral traditions. He argued that myths from 12 different Western Shoshone groups all had underlying commonalities. In the myths, the principal animal character, Coyote, attained manhood by successfully slaying a mountain sheep. It was only after his success in hunting bighorn that Coyote was able to marry. Therefore, it appears that the bighorn was a symbol of male hunting success and had a key association with rites of passage into adulthood.

Rituals prerequisite to the hunting of bighorn sheep are also attested to in Numic myths. Shoshone oral traditions recount Rat's invitation to Mountain

Sheep to join him in the Round Dance. Through his charade, as played out in song, Rat attempted to woo Mountain Sheep to his side, in order to slay him (Lowie 1924a:194-195; Steward 1943:284-285). A Northern Paiute pre-hunt dance and song were traditionally performed by animal-human spirits: Crow, Eagle, Wildcat, Yellow-hammer, and Big Rat (Lowie 1924b:214; Vander 1997:220). These supernaturals danced and sang a song saying, "I am going to shoot mountain sheep."

A puberty rite is ethnographically described in which Numic boys were required to kill a mountain sheep, deer, or pronghorn as a mark of their formal entrance into adulthood (Steward 1941:256). Myers (1997) identified distinctive and recurring relationships between hunting big game animals and human sexual reproduction. He argued that to reach male maturity and be permitted to copulate with women, it was necessary to hunt and kill big game animals.

Northern Paiute ritualist doctors dreamed of "mountain sheep which gave power to suck out and blow away disease" (Steward 1941:259). The Southern Paiute had "game-dreamer" songs and dances that had special importance in hunting bighorn sheep. These "dreamer-singers" would dream about killing game, foods eaten by bighorn sheep, rocky places, rain, bows and arrows, and sometimes "arrows turning into male mountain sheep" (Kelly and Fowler 1986:384-385). In the dreams, a bighorn sheep song was provided as a gift from the sheep. The songs were intended as a means of enhancing the killing of game, and game animals became attracted and increased in number with the proliferation of game food furnished by the rain. The rain, in essence, brought the game.

In her discussion of Chemehuevi shamanism, Kelly (1936:138-142) similarly identified a class of ritual specialists known as sheep dreamers, who were especially adept at charming game animals for the hunt (Hedges 2001:131). The sheep dreamers/game charmers had visions of rain, and bullroarers, and they wore a cap of mountain sheep hide. The cap, fashioned of sheep skin and quail topknots, was a fashionable headpiece for a chief and was reserved for the most skillful hunters of big game animals (Kelly and Fowler 1986:372, Figure 2; Laird 1974, 1976). Kelly (1936:139, 142) further noted that "It is said that rain falls when a mountain sheep is killed. Because of this some mountain-sheep dreamers (i.e., game charmers) thought they were rain doctors."

For the Chemehuevi, a mountain sheep was a good spirit familiar and was exclusively associated with curing shamans (Laird 1976:32-38, 1984). Laird (1976:11) noted that "the mountain sheep and the deer differ from all other animals: they are the only animals who were not shamans in the mythic period, yet appear as shamans' familiars in this present time." Similarly, for the Nevada Shoshone, ritualists dreaming of mountain sheep had the power to cure disease (Steward 1941:259).

Some traditional Numic songs were employed as a means to lure and attract large game animals. By singing songs, a ritualist could capture the souls of the animals and draw power from them. By singing and speaking over the animals and dancing in imitation of their movements, the animals were more easily killed and were already tired and docile when the hunters finally met up with their quarry (Sapir 2002:212; Vander 1997:221, 487). Some Southern Paiute bands would sing to attract sheep, or have a feast and gather around the singer in a partial circle. They would lay bows across their bellies and drape their arms over them, bending their arms and holding their fingers in front of them, representing sheep hooves, and marking time to the music. They also had dancers who would jump and mimic bighorn sheep behavior. These mountain sheep dreamer-singers would direct hunters to the place where they could hunt and slay the sheep. The bighorn song was one of the four principal songs of the Southern Paiute (Laird 1976, 1984).

A core belief of some foraging peoples is that there is innate power in the skeletal remains of hunted animals (Brown 2005; Hultkrantz 1981, 1987a, 1987b). The sacred skulls were believed to be alive, in that they embodied energies associated with animal ancestors. Hence, the animal skull was full of power. The planting or disposal of a deceased animal's bones assured the regeneration process. Great Basin indigenous peoples shared a worldview regarding large game animals that was summarized by Fowler (1986:95):

> . . . respect was shown for animals and plants taken to meet human needs. Portions of larger game animals, including the eyes, skulls, and sometimes organs . . . were specifically set out in the brush or trees or buried after a kill. In addition to showing respect, these acts were a form of manipulation that would insure that game would be continually supplied. Slain game animals were often placed with their heads to the east and addressed with special terminology, again to show respect.

Great Basin Cosmology, Animal Taxonomy, and Bighorn Sheep Religious Symbolism

A brief description of Great Basin cosmology is significant for this discussion. The indigenous view is that the world is ordered into three distinct strata divided into upper, middle, and lower realms that were seeded by different forms of Animal People. Native taxonomy categorizes these animals according to their environment and behavior, or habitats and habits (Vander 1997:155). As such, the religious ecology of the bighorn is central to our analysis.

Having its habitat in the elevated crests of the high, rugged mountains, bighorn sheep typically occupy the uppermost frame in the minds of native Great Basin people (cf. Goss 1972; Myers 1997:44; Nissen 1995:72). Myers (1997:44) affirmed this specific positioning based on analysis of 25 variants of Numic origin myths, and concluded that mountain sheep serve as a topmost symbol due to their association with mountain peaks.

The tiered Great Basin cosmos attributes the color white to the uppermost sky realm (portrayed by snow, clouds, smoke, and fog). As one goes higher in elevation, each division apparently increases in spiritual content and supernatural strength. Goss (1972) argued that the bighorn was identified in Ute worldview as the shamanistic "boss" of the ungulates, and the term for bighorn is applied throughout the Great Basin as a singular reference for all large game animals (cf. Nissen 1995:72).

Goss (1972:126) further emphasized the bighorn's significance by noting that it is the most difficult large game animal to kill, lives in high, rough country, and has a "white rump." The color white is notable, as it is recognized as having the most sacred and highest supernatural status. White is associated with the topmost animal of the sky—the Eagle, the boss of the sky (Goss 1972:126). The color white is also identified with the undersides of the eagle's wings and tail feathers, is considered a symbol of the highest good, and has ritual associations with healing, curing, hunting, shamanism, and vision questing (cf. Miller 1983:70). Hence, the power and energy of the universe is often concentrated in these uppermost planes on mountains and high places—the sites of vision quests and homes of immortals (Miller 1983:70). Therefore, birds soaring above the land are considered metaphoric representatives of the flying and hovering attributes of spiritual energy or power (*puha*). Similarly, it could be argued that the bighorn, abiding just slightly lower than its avian comrades, is imbued with nearly as much kinetic, supernatural, religious power.

Interpreting the Rose Spring Bighorn Sheep Feature

As noted above, several archaeological features and isolated skeletal elements that represent caching and interment of select mountain sheep bones have been discovered in the Desert West. Numic oral traditions provide a context for the possible symbolic import of bighorn faunal caching. The particular importance of the bighorn and the metaphoric content of the burial of their bones are of relevance to an understanding of the cosmology of the indigenous peoples of the West.

Some of the cached elements of these features, such as the skull and atlas bones, contain low meat mass and would be unlikely to represent simple provisioning. Such elements should normally have been left near the kill site rather than being lugged back to a base camp setting. The identification of bighorn crania as trophy skulls could imply that these were symbols of a successful hunt, but their hidden and cached context argues against a simple status symbol or symbolic representation of big game hunting success. As such, it is argued here that, for the most part, these bighorn faunal caches are likely ritual in nature.

The Rose Spring bighorn feature dates to a time (ca. A.D. 500) when many researchers have asserted that Coso Range hunters were drastically depleting local bighorn populations in the immediate area (Garfinkel et al. 2010; Gilreath 2007; Gilreath and Hildebrandt 2008).[2] Rather than switch their prey, as optimal foraging theory would predict, they apparently made bighorn sheep the central focus of large-scale ceremonial activities (Garfinkel 2006; Hildebrandt and McGuire 2002, 2003; McGuire and Hildebrandt 2005). This emphasis on Coso bighorn exploitation may have provided successful hunters with high levels of status and prestige. On the other hand, the interrelationships of religion, hunting, and prestige may have led to ever more intensive hunting efforts resulting in extreme resource depletions (cf. Raven 1990).

A recent computer simulation and review of archaeofaunal data for the Coso region (Figure 8) provides a chronological trajectory for this pattern of Coso bighorn sheep resource depression (Garfinkel et al. 2010). The Rose Spring mountain sheep feature was fashioned during a time when bighorn were undergoing significant population depletions.[3] This occurred close to the inception of bow and arrow use and during a peak period of Coso Representational rock drawing production. It is apparent that the prehistoric inhabitants of the Coso Range experienced a cultural-symbolic fluorescence associated with an intense episode of naturalistic rock art depictions, and this activity may have been accompanied by elaborate ceremonialism and heightened ritual activity.

It has been noted that during tumultuous periods, especially in preliterate cultures, religious rituals become pervasive. Anthropologists have asserted that in stressful times, foraging cultures are especially prone to conduct ceremonies aimed at appeasing and pleasing various spirits and supernaturals (Helventson and Hodgson 2010:65). When events are unpredictable and economic insecurity prevails, ritualistic behaviors have been shown to flourish (Zusne and Jones 1989). The Rose Spring mountain sheep rock cairn and fire pit may have been one physical manifestation of such intense ceremonial activity.

The Rose Spring feature may have been constructed and/or used in association with a bighorn sheep hunt. This might have occurred at any time of the year, but the most frequent period of bighorn hunting (with the best chance of acquiring a large number of animals) was during the fall rutting season, when these animals aggregate and are less wary due to their focus on mating.

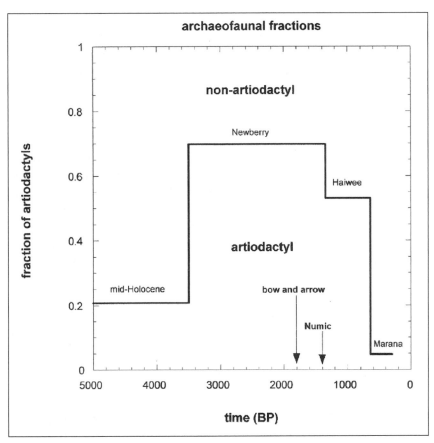

Figure 8. Graph showing the relative frequency of artiodactyl archaeofaunal remains in Coso region prehistoric sites relating to changes over time, including the introduction of the bow and arrow and the possible in-migration of Numic people into the Coso Range.

Referents in religious rituals and oral traditions imply that bighorn sheep were not just something good to eat, but also something to be employed as symbols with multiple, imbricated meanings. In one sense, the bighorn sheep was a religious symbol, an animal immortal, one of the more heralded and sacred figures in Great Basin cosmology. In Numic ideology, the bighorn appears to have represented the entire category of large game animals and was closely related to the hunt, the killing of big game, and the provisioning of meat that evinced heightened status and male hunting prowess. These animals also exhibited close associations with the concepts of prestige, power, and strength, and acted as referents to the men's coming-of-age ceremony and sexual maturity.

The hunting of mountain sheep, the butchering of the slain animals, and the selective disposal of bighorn remains may have been subject to significant ritual and religious rites. Based on limited archaeological data, such meanings may have been applied to bighorn sheep across many millennia of prehistory throughout the Desert West.

Acknowledgments

The authors wish to thank several individuals whose insight and comments were beneficial to the development of a Society for California Archaeology presentation that became the basis for this paper. Included in this group are Alexander K. Rogers, Jill K. Gardner, and Judith Vander. We further appreciate Jill's editing of an earlier draft of this manuscript. We also thank AECOM for their support of this project. Mark Scop assisted with some of the graphics, and Michael Chittock provided the illustration of the sheep "shrine." All errors are the fault of the authors and no one else.

Notes

1. This paper is an attempt to provide a contextual understanding of the possible meaning and function for an unusual feature found at the Rose Spring site at the southwestern edge of the Great Basin. In large measure, we attempt to frame the subject of bighorn ceremonialism in the Desert West using linkages between the ethnographic record and archaeological phenomena. These relationships and connections certainly suffer from a potential temporal/chronological disconnect.

   Almost every archaeological example we use dates to the Middle Archaic, including the Rose Spring site sheep shrine itself. The archaeological expressions noted in this article most frequently predate the presence of Numic speakers. The bighorn sheep headdress we mention could be Numic or might be from a Fremont context. Most people think that Northern proto-Uto Aztecan spread across the southern Great Basin at about 2,500 B.P., with the Takic languages splitting off for southern California soon thereafter, Tubatulabal remaining as a linguistic isolate (or recently reclassified as a remnant Takic member; see Sutton 2010) with Numic splitting from Hopic later, and spreading across the Great Basin relatively late in time.

   The cultural-ethnic distance between the archaeological examples presented in this article and Numic is documented by the ancient DNA record, as the more northerly examples (e.g., Young et al. 2009) probably belong to the haplogroup D population (Kaestle and Smith 2001) or ancestral Washo/Martis (Wilson 1963)—both of which can easily be distinguished from Numic. This is also the case for Fremont skeletal material which is, not surprisingly, more tightly linked to the Anasazi/Pueblo groups.

   It is important to note that sheep hunting is less important in Numic-aged sites than older ones, and ethnographic Numic people do not appear to have fashioned the Coso Representational sheep petroglyphs. However, the Numa were apparently responsible for the very late dating (historic) Coso pictographs representing expressions of the Coso Painted Rock Art Style that incorporates many representational elements, including those regularly depicting bighorn sheep (Garfin-kel et al. 2007).

We are providing information here that shows that there exists a native indigenous symbol-ic focus on bighorn sheep that is widespread in the Desert West and is not necessarily specifically related to the Numa. It is perhaps better seen as representing a deeper, more ancient, associa-tion with aboriginal populations of proto- or pre-Numic, Northern Uto-Aztecan affiliation. The fact that Numic myths often address sheep probably shows how important these animals were to these people, given that the Numic did not appear to hunt them as much as earlier cultures and did not craft as significant a corpus of rock art depicting bighorn sheep.

2. Bighorn depletion appears to have been a local (Coso region) manifestation of resource depression and, of course, the relative importance of bighorn hunting in the Desert West varied by locality. However, prehistorians largely agree that bighorn sheep exploitation did drop off rather dramati-cally after the early Rose Spring era (ca A.D. 300–1000). Numic culture exhibited only limited evidence of the former "bighorn religion." However, hunting of bighorn sheep certainly did not stop; yet, it surely declined from its earlier peak expression but may have come back somewhat after its dramatic fall-off in Rose Spring times (see Garfinkel et al. [2010] for a fuller treatment of this subject).

3. An important part of understanding bighorn ceremonialism in eastern California is the character, sequence, and cultural context of the large-scale changes that took place in the Coso region during the Haiwee Period (ca. A.D. 300–1300). Evidence has been presented elsewhere to support the no-tion that the Coso region experienced a series of prehistoric human population movements and associated radical shifts in adaptive strategies, exchange patterns, and ideological systems during this time (Garfinkel 2006, 2007; Sutton et al. 2007). These changes include the abandonment/popu-lation replacement of pre-Numic populations fostered by the in-migration of the Numic (ca. A.D. 600-1000) into eastern California with pre-Numic people outcompeted by the more labor-inten-sive Numic adaptive strategies (cf. Bettinger and Baumhoff 1982). In-migration of the Numic may have been facilitated by the introduction of the bow and arrow that replaced the earlier dart and atlatl technology (cf. Yohe 1992, 1997). Ensuing competition for subsistence resources (conflicting landscape use), disruption of the trans-Sierran Coso obsidian trade, depletion of big game, and epic droughts (e.g., the Medieval Climatic Anomaly; see Gardner [2007] and references therein) all fac-tored into the transformative changes identified in the Coso region during this eventful time span.

References

Allen, Mark W.
    2011   Of Earth and Stone: Landscape Archaeology in the Mojave Desert. *California Archaeology* 3:11–30.

Bennyhoff, James A., and Richard E. Hughes
    1987   *Shell Bead and Ornament Exchange Networks Between California and the Western Great Basin.* Anthropological Papers of the American Museum of Natural History 64:79–175.

Bettinger, Robert L., and Martin A. Baumhoff
    1982   The Numic Spread: Great Basin Cultures in Competition. *American Antiquity* 47:485–503.

Bolton, Herbert E.
    1930   *Anza's California Expeditions, II*. University of California Press, Berkeley.

Brown, Linda A.
  2005   Planting the Bones: Hunting Ceremonialism at Contemporary and Nineteenth-Century
            Shrines in the Guatemala Highlands. *Latin American Antiquity* 16:131–146.
Castetter, Edward F., and Willis H. Bell
  1942   *Pima and Papago Indian Agriculture* (1st ed.). University of New Mexico Press, Albuquerque.
Castetter, Edward F., and Ruth M. Underhill
  1935   *Ethnobiological Studies in the American Southwest II: The Ethnobiology of the Papago Indians.*
            University of New Mexico Bulletin 4:1–84.
Coulam, Nancy J., and A. R. Schroedl
  2004   Late Archaic Totemism in the Greater American Southwest. *American Antiquity* 69:41–62.
Davis, C. Alan, and Gerald Smith
  1981   *Newberry Cave.* San Bernardino County Museum Association Special Publication, Red-
            lands.
Earle, David D.
  2000   Accounts of the Sand Canyon Region Collected from Native Elders at the Tejon Rancheria.
            Antelope Valley Archaeological Society Newsletter 30(9):4–6.
Fowler, Catherine S.
  1986   Subsistence. In *Great Basin*, edited by Warren L. d'Azevedo, pp. 466–498. Handbook of
            North American Indians, Vol. 11, William C. Sturtevant, general editor. Smithsonian
            Institution, Washington, D.C.
Gardner, Jill K.
  2007   *The Potential Impact of the Medieval Climatic Anomaly on Human Populations in the Western
            Mojave Desert.* Coyote Press Archives of Great Basin Prehistory, No. 7.
Garfinkel, Alan P.
  2006   Paradigm Shifts, Rock Art Theory, and the Coso Sheep Cult of Eastern California. *North
            American Archaeologist* 27:203–244.
  2007   *Archaeology and Rock Art of the Eastern Sierra and Great Basin Frontier.* Maturango Museum
            Publication No. 22, Ridgecrest, California.
Garfinkel, Alan, and Donald R. Austin
  2011   Reproductive Symbolism in Great Basin Rock Art: Bighorn Sheep Hunting, Fertility, and
            Forager Ideology. *Cambridge Archaeological Journal* 21:453–471.
Garfinkel, Alan P., and Robert M. Yohe, II
  2002   Antiquity and Function: Humboldt Basal-notched Bifaces in the Southwestern Great
            Basin. *Journal of California and Great Basin Anthropology* 24:103–125.
Garfinkel, Alan P., Geron Marcom, and Robert A. Schiffman
  2007   Culture Crisis and Rock Art Intensification: Numic Ghost Dance Paintings and Coso Rep-
            resentational Petroglyphs. *American Indian Rock Art*, Vol. 33, edited by Don Christensen
            and Peggy Whitehead, pp. 83–103. American Rock Art Research Association, Tucson,
            Arizona.
Garfinkel, Alan P., David A. Young, and Robert M. Yohe, II
  2010   Bighorn Hunting, Resource Depression, and Rock Art in the Coso Range of Eastern Cali-
            fornia: A Computer Simulation Model. *Journal of Archaeological Science* 37:42–51.
Garfinkel, Alan P., Donald R. Austin, David Earle, and Harold Williams
  2009   Myth, Ritual, and Rock Art: Coso Decorated Animal-Humans and the Animal Master. *Rock
            Art Research* 26:179–197.

Geist, Valerius, and R. G. Petocz
  1977   Bighorn Sheep in Winter: Do Rams Maximize Reproductive Fitness by Spatial and Habitat
          Segregation from Ewes? *Canadian Journal of Zoology* 55:1802–1810.
Gilmore, Harry W.
  1953   Hunting Habits of the Early Nevada Paiutes. *American Anthropologist* 55:148–153.
Gilreath, Amy J.
  2007   Rock Art in the Golden State: Pictographs and Petroglyphs, Portable and Panoramic. In
          California Prehistory: Colonization, Culture and Complexity, edited by Terry L. Jones and
          Kathryn A. Klar, pp. 273–290. AltaMira, Lanham, Maryland.
Gilreath, Amy J., and William R. Hildebrandt
  2008   Coso Rock Art Within Its Archaeological Context. *Journal of California and Great Basin
          Anthropology* 28:1–22.
Goss, James A.
  1972   A Basin-Plateau Shoshonean Ecological Model. *Desert Research Institute Publications in
          Social Sciences* 8:123–128. University of Nevada Press, Reno.
Grant, Campbell
  1980   The Desert Bighorn and Aboriginal Man. In *The Desert Bighorn: Its Life History, Ecology and
          Management*, edited by Gale Monson and Lowell Sumner, pp. 7–39. University of Arizona
          Press, Tucson.
Grant, Campbell, James W. Baird, and J. Kenneth Pringle
  1968   *Rock Drawings of the Coso Range, Inyo County, California: An Ancient Sheep-Hunting Cult
          Pictured in Desert Rock Carvings*. Maturango Museum Publication No. 4, Ridgecrest, Cali-
          fornia.
Hansen, Charles C., and O. V. Deming
  1980   Growth and Development. In *The Desert Bighorn: Its Life History, Ecology and Management*,
          edited by Gale Monson and Lowell Sumner, pp. 152–171. University of Arizona Press,
          Tucson.
Harrington, John Peabody
  1986   *Ethnographic Field Notes, Volume 3, Southern California/Basin*. Smithsonian Institution,
          National Anthropological Archives, Washington. (Microfilm edition, Millwood, New York).
Hedges, Ken
  2001   Traversing the Great Gray Middle Ground: An Examination of Shamanistic Interpreta-
          tion of Rock Art. In *American Indian Rock Art* 27, edited by Steven M. Freers and Alanah
          Woody, pp. 123–136. American Rock Art Research Association, Tucson.
Helventson, Patricia A., and Derek Hodgson
  2010   The Neuropsychology of "Animism": Implications for Understanding Rock Art. *Rock Art
          Research* 27:43–60.
Hildebrandt, William R., and Kelly R. McGuire
  2002   The Ascendance of Hunting during the California Middle Archaic: An Evolutionary Per-
          spective. *American Antiquity* 67:231–256.
  2003   Large-Game Hunting, Gender-Differentiated Work Organization, and the Role of Evo-
          lutionary Ecology in California and Great Basin Prehistory: A Reply to Broughton and
          Bayham. *American Antiquity* 68:790–792.
Hultkrantz, Åke
  1981   Accommodation and Persistence: Ecological Analysis of the Religion of the Sheepeater
          Indians in Wyoming, U.S.A. *Temenos: Studies in Comparative Religion* 17:35–44.

1986a   Mythology and Religious Concepts. In *Great Basin*, edited by Warren L. d'Azevedo, pp. 630–640. Handbook of North American Indians, Vol. 11, William C. Sturtevant. general editor. Smithsonian Institution, Washington, D.C.

1986b   Rock Drawings as Evidence of Religion: Some Principal Points of View. In *Words and Objects: Towards a Dialogue between Archaeology and History of Religion*, edited by Gro Steinsland, pp. 42–66. The Institute for Comparative Research in Human Culture, Norwegian University Press, Oslo, and Oxford University Press, New York.

1987a   *Native Religions of North America*. Harper and Row, San Francisco.

1987b   Diversity in Cosmology. *Canadian Journal of Native Studies* 7:279–295.

Husted, Wilfred M., and Robert Edgar

2002   *The Archaeology of Mummy Cave, Wyoming: An Introduction to Shoshonean Prehistory*. National Park Service, Midwest Archeological Center Special Report No. 4 and Southeast Archaeological Center Technical Reports Series No. 9.

Kaestle, Frederika A., and David G. Smith

2001   Ancient Mitochondrial DNA Evidence for Prehistoric Population Movement: The Numic Expansion. *American Journal of Physical Anthropology* 115:1–12.

Kelly, Isabel T.

1936   Chemehuevi Shamanism. In *Essays in Anthropology Presented to A. L. Kroeber in Celebration of his Sixtieth Birthday*, edited by Robert Lowie, pp. 129–142. University of California Press, Berkeley.

Kelly, Isabel T., and Catherine S. Fowler

1986   Southern Paiute. In *Great Basin*, edited by Warren L. d'Azevedo, pp. 368–397. Handbook of North American Indians, Vol. 11, William C. Sturtevant, general editor. Smithsonian Institution, Washington, D.C.

King, Chester D.

1990   *Evolution of Chumash Society: A Comparative Study of Artifacts Used for Social System Maintenance in the Santa Barbara Channel Region Before A.D. 1804*. Garland Publishing, New York.

Laird, Carobeth

1974   Chemehuevi Religious Beliefs and Practices. *Journal of California Anthropology* 1:19–25.

1976   *The Chemehuevis*. Malki Museum, Banning.

1984   *Mirror and Pattern: George Laird's World of Chemehuevi Mythology*. Malki Museum, Banning.

Lowie, Robert H.

1924a   Shoshonean Tales. *Journal of American Folklore* 37:1–242.

1924b   *Primitive Religion*. Bonni and Liveright, New York.

Malouf, Carling S.

1966   Ethnohistory in the Great Basin. In *The Current Status of Anthropological Research in the Great Basin: 1964*, edited by Warren L. d'Azevedo, Wilbur A. Davis, Don D. Fowler, and Wayne Suttles, pp. 1–38. Desert Research Institute Social Sciences and Humanities Publication 1, University of Nevada, Reno.

Matheny, Ray T., Thomas S. Smith, and Deanne G. Matheny

1997   Animal Ethology Reflected in the Rock Art of Nine Mile Canyon, Utah. *Journal of California and Great Basin Anthropology* 19:70–103.

McGuire, Kelly R., and William R. Hildebrandt

2005   Re-Thinking Great Basin Foragers: Prestige Hunting and Costly Signaling during the Middle Archaic Period. *American Antiquity* 70:695–712.

Miller, Jay

    1983   Basin Religion and Theology: Comparative Study of Power (*Puha*). *Journal of California and Great Basin Anthropology* 5:66–86.

Myers, Daniel L.

    1997   Animal Symbolism Among the *Numa*: Symbolic Analysis of Numic Origin Myths. *Journal of California and Great Basin Anthropology* 19:32–97.

Nissen, Karen M.

    1995   Prey for Signs? Petroglyph Research in Western Great Basin of North America. In *Rock Art Studies in the Americas: Papers from the Darwin Rock Art Congress* edited by Jack Steinberg, pp. 67–76. Oxbow Monograph 45, Oxbow Books, Great Britain.

Park, Willard Z.

    1941   Cultural Succession in the Great Basin. In *Language, Culture and Personality: Essays in Memory of Edward Sapir*, edited by Leslie Sapir, A. I. Halowell, and Stanley S. Newman, pp. 180–203. Sapir Memorial Publication Fund, Menasha, Wisconsin.

Raven, Michelle M.

    1990   The Point of No Diminishing Returns: Hunting and Resource Decline on Boigu Island, Torres Strait. Unpublished Ph.D. dissertation, Department of Anthropology, University of California, Davis.

Sapir, Edward

    2002   *Edward Sapir: The Psychology of Culture, A Course of Lectures* (2nd edition). Reconstructed and edited by Judith T. Irvine. Mouton de Gruyter, Berlin.

Shimkin, Demitri B.

    1970   Sociocultural Persistence among Shoshoneans of the Carson River Basin (Nevada). In *Language and Cultures of Western North America: Essays in Honor of Sven S. Liljeblad*, edited by Earl H. Swanson Jr., pp. 172–199. Idaho State University Press, Pocatello.

Steward, Julian H.

    1941   Cultural Element Distributions: XIII, Nevada Shoshone. *University of California Anthropological Records* 4(2).

    1943   Some Western Shoshoni Myths. *Bureau of American Ethnology Bulletin* 136.

    1968   Forward. In Rock Drawings of the Coso Range: An Ancient Sheep-Hunting Cult Pictured in Desert Rock Carvings, by Campbell Grant, James W. Baird, and J. Kenneth Pringle, pp. vii–x. *Maturango Museum Publications* No. 4, Ridgecrest, California.

Stewart, Omer C.

    1941   Culture Element Distributions XIV: Northern Paiute. *University of California Anthropological Records* 4:361–446.

Sutton, Mark Q.

    1981   Bighorn Sheep Rock Art from the Southern Sierra Nevada. *Masterkey* 55(1):13–17.

    1982   Kawaiisu Mythology and Rock Art: One Example. *Journal of California and Great Basin Anthropology* 4:148–154.

    2001   Excavations at Teddy Bear Cave (CA-KER-508), Tomo Kahni State Park, Southern Sierra Nevada, California. *Pacific Coast Archaeological Society Quarterly* 37(1):1–26.

    2010   A Reevaluation of Early Northern Uto-Aztecan Prehistory in Alta California. *California Archaeology* 2:3–30.

Sutton, Mark Q., and Robert M. Yohe II

    1987   Nopah Cave: A Late Period Sheep Hunting Camp in the Southwestern Great Basin. *Pacific Coast Archaeological Society Quarterly* 23(3):24–34.

Sutton, Mark Q., Mark E. Basgall, Jill K. Gardner, and Mark W. Allen
    2007   Advances in Understanding Mojave Desert Prehistory. In *California Prehistory: Coloniza-
            tion, Culture and Complexity*, edited by Terry L. Jones and Kathryn A. Klar, pp. 229–246.
            AltaMira Press, Lanham, Maryland.
Vander, Judith
    1997   *Shoshone Ghost Dance Religion: Poetry Songs and Great Basin Context*. University of Illinois
            Press, Chicago.
Van Tilburg, Jo Anne, Gordon E. Hull, and John C. Bretney (editors)
    2012   *Captured Visions*. Cotsen Institute of Archaeology at the University of California, Los
            Angeles.
Whitley, David S.
    1982   Notes on the Coso Petroglyphs, the Etiological Mythology of the Western Shoshone,
            and the Interpretation of Rock Art. *Journal of California and Great Basin Anthropology*
            4:262–272.
    1998   Meaning and Metaphor in the Coso Petroglyphs: Understanding Great Basin Rock Art. In
            Coso Rock Art: A New Perspective, Elva Younkin, editor, pp. 109–176. Maturango Museum
            Publication No. 12, Ridgecrest, California.
Wilson, Norman L.
    1963   The Archaeology of the Loyalton Rock Shelter, Sierra County, California. Unpublished
            Master's thesis, Department of Anthropology, California State University, Sacramento.
Yohe, Robert M., II
    1992   A Reevaluation of Western Great Basin Cultural Chronology and Evidence for the Timing
            of the Introduction of the Bow and Arrow to Eastern California Based on New Excavations
            at the Rose Spring Site (CA-INY-372). Unpublished Ph.D. dissertation, Department of
            Anthropology, University of California, Riverside.
    1997   The Introduction of the Bow and Arrow and Lithic Resource Use at Rose Spring (CA-
            INY-372). *Journal of California and Great Basin Anthropology* 20:26–52.
Young, D. Craig, William R. Hildebrandt, Steven D. Neidig, and Sharon A. Waechter
    2009   Report from Fish Springs to Dry Valley: Archaeological Investigations on the Vidler Water
            Project Corridor, Washoe County, Nevada. Report on file at Far Western Anthropological
            Research Group, Davis, California.
Zigmond, Maurice L.
    1977   The Supernatural World of the Kawaiisu. In *Flowers of the Wind: Papers on Ritual, Myth,
            and Symbolism in California and the Southwest*, edited by Thomas C. Blackburn, pp. 59–95.
            Ballena Press Anthropological Papers No. 8, Socorro, New Mexico.
    1980   *Kawaiisu Mythology, An Oral Tradition of South-Central California*. Ballena Press Anthropo-
            logical Papers No. 18.
Zusne, Leonard, and Warren H. Jones
    1989   *Anomalistic Psychology: A Study of Magical Thinking*. Lawrence Erlbaum Associates, Hills-
            dale, New Jersey.

Middle Archaic Interaction Spheres Interpreted from Toolstone Distributions in the Tahoe Sierra

William W. Bloomer
Lithic Arts, Woodfords, CA (LithicArts@Hughes.net)

Denise Jaffke
California State Parks, Sierra District (djaffke@parks.ca.gov)

Abstract   Research in the Tahoe Sierra region has defined regional toolstone distribution patterns that give us a glimpse of how lithic source materials were moved over the landscape and addresses larger issues concerning settlement dynamics, population movement, and resource movement by way of prehistoric travel and exchange. Synthesis of prior archaeological investigations in the region and the compilation of larger data sets have allowed us to further identify intraregional distribution patterns that partition the region into three zones and model local interaction spheres based on dominant toolstone type that have implications for continuity in ancestral Washoe land use. Three key Middle Archaic sites situated within these zones serve as case studies that help illustrate the overall patterns. The model presented in this paper builds a framework for future research in the Tahoe Sierra region and provides an interpretative baseline to explain toolstone distribution patterns and a means to understand economics and social dynamics within and beyond the three local interaction spheres.

Resumen   La investigación en la región de Tahoe Sierra ha definido los patrones de distribución regional de materiales líticos que nos dan una idea de como los materiales líticos de fuente se movían sobre el paisaje y ha tradado a las cuestiones más amplias sobre la dinámica de asentamiento, los movimientos de población, y el movimiento de recursos por medio de los viajes y el intercambio prehistóricos. La síntesis de las investigaciones arqueológicas anteriores en la región y la compilación de conjuntos más grandes de datos nos han permitido determinar con más precisión los patrones de la distribución intrarregional que dividen la región en tres zonas y hacer un modelo de ámbitos locales de interacción basado en el tipo dominante de material lítico que tienen implicaciones para la continuidad del uso de la tierra ancestral washoe. Tres sitios clave del Arcaico Medio, situado dentro de estas zonas, sirven como estudios de casos que ayudan

California Archaeology, Volume 4, Number 2, December 2012, pp. 225–246.

a ilustrar los patrones generales. El modelo presentado en este artículo crea un marco para la investigación futura en la región de Tahoe Sierra y proporciona un punto de referencia interpretativa para explicar los patrones de distribución de la materia lítica y un medio para entender la economía y la dinámica social dentro y fuera de las tres esferas locales de interacción.

Toolstone distribution is a productive area of study for archaeologists working in the Lake Tahoe area of the northern Sierra Nevada (referred to here as the Tahoe Sierra Region; Figure 1). This is fortunate because the region generally lacks stratigraphic deposits while poor organic preservation limits the potential for both faunal analysis and radiocarbon dating. Due to these inherent limitations,

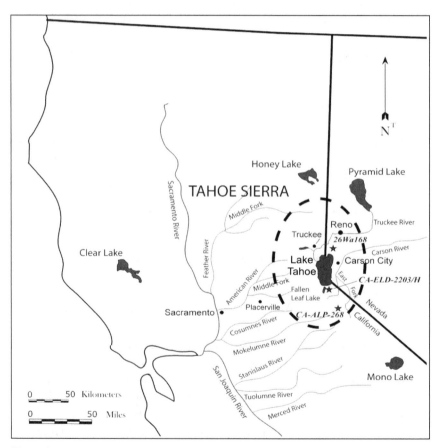

Figure 1. The Tahoe Sierra Region.

current research on land use patterns based on toolstone distributions with time control inferred from obsidian hydration has proven fruitful.

Here we demonstrate how toolstone composition and hydration data can be linked to infer land use patterns at the regional level. We offer a land use model for the Tahoe Sierra Region that illustrates how different groups moved about the landscape around Lake Tahoe. The model was developed with data from three important Middle Archaic sites that exemplify distinctive toolstone patterns that exist throughout the region. The toolstone composition at these sites reflects intraregional variability in the geologic availability of toolstone, as well as variability in toolstone procurement by the human populations that inhabited the sites. The toolstone composition at each site indicates a trenchant toolstone procurement pattern that we interpret to represent local population interaction spheres.

Key sites for this study include 26Wa168, located in Washoe County, Nevada, on Mt. Rose, 8 km north of Lake Tahoe; CA-ELD-2203/H, located in El Dorado County, California, on Fallen Leaf Lake; and CA-ALP-268, located in Alpine County, California, 30 km southeast of Tahoe along Hot Springs Creek (Figure 1). Original data for each site were compiled as a result of test excavations reported by Bloomer (2003, 2006) and Jaffke and Bloomer (2008). Each of these sites was occupied primarily during the Middle Archaic, after 4,000 B.P. (Table 1). The bulk of the obsidian hydration measurements from these sites ranges between 6.4 and 1.2 microns, indicating initial occupations during the Early Archaic with infrequent use extending into the Late Archaic. Most importantly, hydration means ranging between 4.3 and 3.0 microns (Table 2) place the predominant site occupations squarely within the Middle Archaic from approximately 3,400 B.P. to 1,800 B.P., respectively.

Regional Research Context

Initial toolstone research during the 1970s and 1980s focused on obsidian, using geochemical characterization (Hughes 1986, 1992) to identify sources and interpret interregional exchange networks for the movement of obsidian into the Tahoe Sierra (Markley and Day 1992). Basalt sourcing entered the milieu in the 1990s to study intraregional distributions of basalt toolstone from the numerous basalt quarries located north of Lake Tahoe (Bloomer et al. 1997; Day et al. 1996; Jackson et al. 1994; Latham et al. 1992; Skinner and Davis 1996). The outcome of both obsidian and basalt studies identified roughly north/south and northeast/southwest distribution patterns, generally mirroring the directionality of the geomorphic landforms within the northern Sierra Nevada. The growing evidence for toolstone distribution patterns led to interpretations of toolstone procurement by

Table 1. The Tahoe Sierra Cultural Chronology.

Climatic Period	Adaptive Sequence*	Years B.P.*
	Late Archaic Period	
		1300
Late Holocene		
	Middle Archaic Period	
		4000
Middle Holocene	Early Archaic Period	
		7000
Early Holocene	Pre-Archaic Period	
		10,000
Late Pleistocene	Fluted Point Period	
		> 13,000

* Based on Elston 1986; Elston et al. 1994

population movement and exchange within relatively long distance Tahoe Sierra interaction spheres (McGuire and Bloomer 1997).

Cryptocrystalline silicate (CCS) and metamorphic (metasedimentary and metavolcanic) toolstone sources also occur within the Tahoe Sierra. Metamorphic and CCS toolstone in archaeological assemblages are identified by morphological characteristics such as color and texture. Sourcing each relies on a working knowledge of local geology and the ability to match toolstone characteristics to one or more sources where that kind of toolstone occurs. Metamorphic and CCS source analysis contributes additional data sets for studying Tahoe Sierra toolstone use and distribution.

Through the years, toolstone source analysis has become standard methodological practice for most prehistoric research in northern California. Accumulating source data provides the foundation for land use studies in current Sierra Nevada research designs (Bloomer and Jaffke 2009a; Lindström et al. 2002). A tenet of hunter-gatherer research is that toolstone procurement was commonly

Table 2. Obsidian Hydration Data for Key Sites in the Tahoe Sierra Area.

Site	Range*	Age Range**	Mean	Mean Age B.P.	SD	CV	Count	Outlier
26Wa168	4.8-1.2	4000–300	3.0	1800	0.9	0.3	146	5.5
CA-ELD-2203/H	5.7-1.2	5300–300	3.5	2400	1.3	0.4	26	—
CA-ALP-268	6.4-1.7	6400–600	4.3	3400	1.1	0.3	27	10.1

* Ranges and means in microns
**Ages are approximate years before present (B.P.)
SD = Standard Deviation; CV = Coefficient of Variation

embedded in subsistence systems and settlement patterns (Binford 1983). Hence, it is widely accepted that toolstone distributions serve as a proxy for population movement and interaction (e.g., Basgall 1989; Basgall and McGuire 1988; Delacorte and McGuire 1993). We believe that this is true and can be applied to toolstone distribution analyses within the Tahoe Sierra.

In essence, people procured toolstone by direct access to the source, transported that toolstone throughout their territory, used it along the way, and eventually exchanged it to others who then continued to move it into adjacent territories and over long distances. Cohesive subsistence/settlement territories, discussed below as "local interaction spheres," are indicated by high percentages of available toolstone in site assemblages. Decreasing frequencies of available toolstone indicate the margins of local interaction spheres, where access to toolstone sources through direct procurement became less common, but the potential for exchange may have increased.

Toolstone procurement and transport solely for the purpose of exchange has not specifically been identified in the Tahoe Sierra. Procurement for exchange may have occurred to a greater extent at the largest basalt quarries, such as Alder Hill, but was likely embedded in a more common pattern of subsistence procurement. On the other hand, because Bodie Hills obsidian is so ubiquitous throughout the Tahoe Sierra, and typically at high frequencies, procurement specifically for exchange was likely a common practice that contributed to Bodie Hills distribution.

Regional Interpretation of Obsidian Hydration

Obsidian hydration data are interpreted chronologically with reference to a hypothetical hydration curve (Figure 2). The curve is based on two anchor points, one at each end of the temporal spectrum. The older end of the curve is anchored by a 7.0 hydration mean associated with a single component pre-Archaic deposit at site

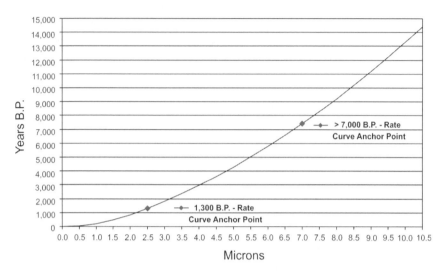

Figure 2. Hypothetical obsidian hydration rate curve for the Tahoe Sierra.

FS 05-19-795 in South Lake Tahoe (Martin 1998). Pre-Archaic deposits typically predate 7,000 B.P.; therefore, the 7.0 micron value is interpreted as greater than 7,000 B.P. and plotted at 7,420 B.P. on the hydration curve. The younger end of the curve is anchored by the 2.5 micron value at the transition from Middle Archaic to Late Archaic (1,300 B.P.), because Late Archaic arrow point hydration data are relatively consistent at less than 2.5 microns. For example, a recent analysis of 32 Rose Spring series projectile points from the Tahoe Sierra showed a 2.2 micron mean, which is interpreted on the hydration curve to correlate with a date of approximately 1,000 B.P.

The hydration curve represents the general trend for obsidian from above the 5,500-ft elevation. The 5,500-ft elevation is significant because from this point and above the hydration rate is noticeably slower than at lower elevations along the western Sierra foothills (cf. Rosenthal and Meyer's [2011:Table 3] preferred A1, C, and D rates for Bodie Hills hydration on the western slope of the north-central Sierra). Chilling temperatures, periodic forest fires, and constant bioturbation of archaeological deposits above 5,500 ft have likely contributed to a variable hydration rate along the general curve. Due to this variability, the hypothetical curve is applied irrespective of the source for most of the obsidian. Obsidian sources that hydrate at much higher rates (e.g., Coso) or much slower rates (e.g., Buffalo Hills) are rarely found in the Tahoe Sierra.

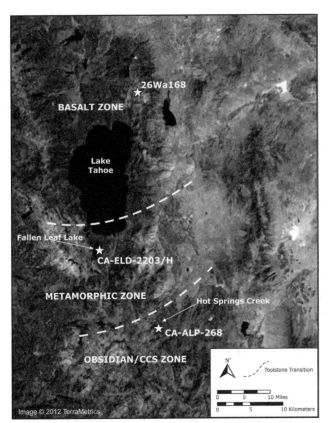

Figure 3. Three geologic toolstone zones in the Tahoe Sierra. The dashed lines indicate transitional boundaries.

Geologic Zones and Toolstone Distribution

Toolstone composition at each of the three sites is largely influenced by geology. It is apparent that toolstone procurement focused on local sources where good toolstone was available. Where not available, toolstone was acquired from more distant sources by direct procurement or exchange. The kinds and sources of toolstone used likely depended on social relationships with neighbors who had access to geologic deposits within and beyond an interaction sphere.

Three geologic toolstone zones occur within the Tahoe area: the basalt zone, the metamorphic zone, and the obsidian/CCS zone (Figure 3). The basalt and metamorphic zones are geographic areas where the toolstone composition at Middle Archaic sites is characterized by high frequencies of the local toolstone. In the case of the obsidian/CCS zone, sites are characterized by low frequencies of local toolstone and a predominance of imported materials. Each zone is represented by a

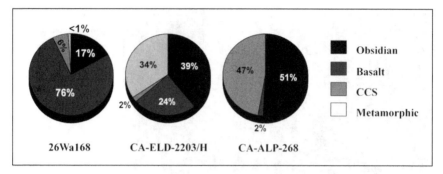

Figure 4. Pie charts comparing toolstone percentages from the three key sites discussed in this article (26Wa168, CA-ELD-2203/H, and CA-ALP-268).

key site. Toolstone frequencies calculated for each key site include the most common toolstone materials only: basalt, obsidian, CCS, and metamorphic (metasedimentary and metavolcanic). Less common flaked stone materials (such as quartz) and groundstone materials are not included.

The basalt zone extends north from Lake Tahoe to the Sierra Valley. This zone is characterized by various Miocene to Pleistocene age andesite and basalt flows (Saucedo 2005; Saucedo and Wagner 1992), evident today as bedrock outcrops and lag deposits. Good quality basalt toolstone sources and quarries are numerous within the basalt zone (Bloomer et al. 1997; Day et al. 1996). Site 26Wa168 is representative of the vast majority of the sites located within the basalt zone, in that basalt is the dominant toolstone. The toolstone assemblage at 26Wa168 is 76% basalt (Figure 4), indicating that basalt sources experienced extensive local use. Non-basalt toolstone is much less frequent and includes 17% obsidian, 6% CCS, and less than 1% metamorphic.

The metamorphic zone occupies a relatively small area, incorporating South Lake Tahoe and extending south to Carson Pass. Metamorphic rock in this zone emanates from several high-elevation geologic areas (Koenig 1963; Saucedo 2005; Wagner et al. 1981). Extensive exposures of good quality toolstone occur as Jurassic age metasedimentary and metavolcanic bedrock south and west of Mt. Tallac, west of Fallen Leaf Lake. An additional bedrock source of metasedimentary toolstone occurs just above the northeast shore of Fallen Leaf Lake on Tahoe Mountain. Other exposures of Triassic to Jurassic age metasedimentary bedrock occur on the high slopes, west and east of the upper reach of the West Fork of the Carson River. Nodules, eroded as lag deposits from these ancient sources, can be found on lower slopes and in drainages throughout the metamorphic zone. Site CA-ELD-2203/H, situated on the northeast shore of Fallen Leaf Lake, typifies sites in the metamorphic zone. Here, metamorphic and obsidian toolstone are nearly equal in frequency at 34% and 39%, respectively (Figure 4). Although not necessarily the dominant toolstone in this zone, metamorphic artifacts are never found at such high frequencies outside the metamorphic zone. Other toolstone recovered from the site include basalt (24%) and CCS (2%), low percentages compared with sites located to the north.

In contrast to the basalt and metamorphic zones, the obsidian/CCS zone is characterized by a lack of local toolstone. Local sources of basalt and metamorphic toolstone are limited in this zone, essentially present only as low frequency nodules and small bedrock outcrops. As such, the predominant toolstone at CA-ALP-268 and other sites within the obsidian/CCS zone is obsidian, with equal or somewhat lesser frequencies of CCS (Figure 4). Obsidian (51%) and most of the CCS (47%) toolstone were imported. Opalitic wood was available in small quantities along the Sierra Crest to the west (Frazetti and Morris 2008; Maher and Blom 1999), while siliceous rhyolite and other CCS deposits have limited availability in small pockets within the Pliocene volcanic flows of the eastern Sierra front (Koenig 1963; Shapiro 2010). More importantly, sedimentary chert was only available at greater distances as alluvial and colluvial cobbles within Quaternary deposits in the south Carson Valley, Smith Valley, and the Pine Nut Range to the east (Moore 1969).

Toolstone Transport and Interaction Spheres

These toolstone zones define the geologic and geographic contexts within which toolstone procurement and use was affected. The transport of toolstone from specific sources to each of the key sites within each zone demonstrates the interaction sphere of people occupying those sites as part of their routine seasonal land use within the larger regional Middle Archaic interaction sphere. Each of the key sites is viewed as a central place in a land use strategy. Because these sites are at high elevations, they were likely utilized seasonally. The obsidian hydration data show that occupations were repetitive throughout the Middle Archaic. Site use may have been relatively long-term from spring through fall, and possibly even year-round during periods of climatic warming.

Site 26Wa168 yielded the largest flaked stone assemblage in the current study, with a sample of 61 basalt and 102 obsidian specimens submitted for geochemical analysis. Thus, the 26Wa168 data are the most diverse and robust for identifying a local interaction sphere. Of the three key sites, 26Wa168 provides the best example of the potential for toolstone research through geochemical source analysis. Toolstone samples from the other two sites are less robust, but still offer real contrasts in toolstone procurement that support the distinction of local interaction spheres.

26Wa168

Site 26Wa168 is a residential camp sitting at 2,854 m (9,360 ft) in elevation in a glacial cirque by a pond at the head of the upper Third Creek drainage on the southern flanks of Mt. Rose. The moderate size of the site (ca. 12,000 m²) incorporates two separate artifact concentrations, surrounded and connected by a generally sparse background artifact scatter. Bedrock milling slicks and portable milling slabs are abundant throughout the site. Flaked stone artifacts are also abundant and diverse, including relatively large quantities of projectile

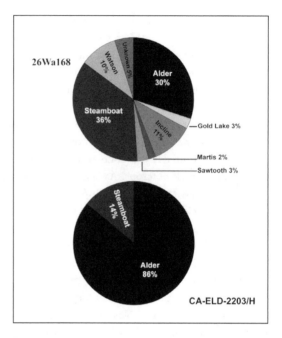

Figure 5. Pie charts comparing basalt percentages from two of the key sites (26Wa168 and CA-ELD-2203/H).

points, bifaces, and debitage, with less frequent occurrences of unifaces, edge-modified flakes, core tools, cores, a grooved abrader, and a hammerstone.

The local interaction sphere for 26Wa168 residents is indicated primarily by basalt (Figure 5) transported from six distinct local sources, with the addition of obsidian (Figure 6) transported from two local sources. Basalt from Steamboat Hills is most frequent at 36% (n = 22). The Steamboat Hills source is located 16 km northeast and at a substantially lower elevation in the eastern foothills of the Carson Range. The Steamboat Hills quarry would have been accessible from winter villages in the Truckee Meadows, south of Reno, and was likely visited seasonally en route to the Tahoe uplands (Figure 7). The presence of Steamboat Hills basalt represents a winter aspect of the land use pattern, incorporating the lower elevation eastern valleys. The winter aspect is further indicated by the presence of Sutro Springs and CB Concrete obsidian at 26Wa168. Sutro Springs was a readily accessible source of small to moderate size nodules located approximately 48 km east, while CB Concrete was a low frequency source of small nodules located a few kilometers northeast of Steamboat Hills. Sutro accounts for 31% (n = 32) of the obsidian sample from the site, while CB Concrete adds another 3% (n = 3). The percentage of obsidian at Sutro Springs is a relatively high frequency in the Tahoe Sierra, indicating regular access to the source.

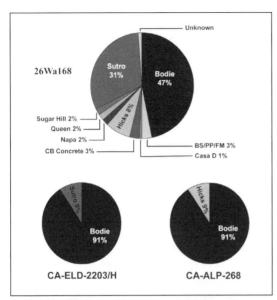

Figure 6. Pie charts comparing obsidian percentages from the three key sites discussed in this article (26Wa168, CA-ELD-2203/H, and CA-ALP-268).

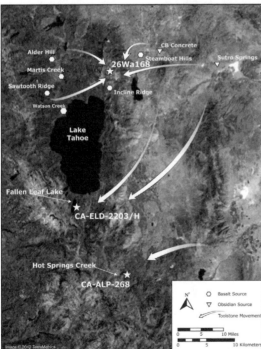

Figure 7. The directionality of toolstone movement in the study area is shown by arrows emanating from sources.

Alder Hill basalt accounts for 30% (n = 18)[1] of the basalt sample at 26Wa168 (Figure 5). Alder Hill is a large and extensively quarried source, with its basalt distributed throughout the Tahoe Sierra. Located only 24 km northwest, Alder Hill sits at the northwestern edge of Martis Valley in proximity to riverine resources along the Truckee River and its tributaries. Movement to the quarry would have facilitated acquisition of multiple seasonally available food resources, as well as toolstone. A small percentage of Martis Creek basalt (2%, n = 1) is also present at 26Wa168, further indicating resource acquisition from Martis Valley.

Transport of basalt from the Watson Creek source (10%, n = 6) and the Sawtooth Ridge source (3%, n = 2) indicates that population movement from 26Wa168 extended west to the upper reach of the Truckee River and the northwest Tahoe shores. Again, riverine and lacustrine resources were seasonally abundant in the vicinity of both basalt quarries. The fact that the frequencies for both Watson and Sawtooth basalt are relatively low suggests that these quarries were visited less often and are at the furthest extent of the local interaction sphere. Close to the site, within 5 km southeast, Incline Ridge basalt accounts for 11% (n = 7) of the sample. This relatively low frequency is probably due to the fact that Incline Ridge nodules are small with less utility than the larger cobbles and bedrock available at the other sources. Incline Ridge basalt is not often found at sites away from the source, and only at low frequencies.

Basalt toolstone transported from the predominant sources to the site arrived primarily as flake blanks, early stage bifaces, and late stage bifaces. Clearly, 26Wa168 site residents were visiting the quarries to procure basalt toolstone for tool manufacture. Most of the on-site basalt biface reduction was concerned with late stage percussion biface thinning and pressure shaping to make bifacial tools for use. Finished tools were likely exchanged within and beyond the local interaction sphere for non-local resources, trade goods, and tools made of toolstone from distant sources.

The local interaction sphere of people living seasonally at 26Wa168, represented by basalt and obsidian source data, encompasses an approximately 1,400 km^2 area north of Lake Tahoe, trending approximately 70 km east-west from the Carson Valley lowlands to the upper reach of the Truckee River and at least 20 km north from Tahoe's north shore (Figure 8). This high-elevation site is centrally located within the Tahoe Sierra landscape. A short walk to the high western ridge affords a vantage point with 360-degree views. From here, the high ridgeline runs south to Lake Tahoe, through several milling stations and concentrations of flaked stone tools that represent high-elevation task sites. Large Middle Archaic village sites, occupied concurrently with 26Wa168, lie to the west in Martis Valley, where Alder Hill basalt quarry is plainly visible. Ridgelines and steep canyons provide direct travel routes down to Martis Valley. The low valleys of the Truckee Mead-

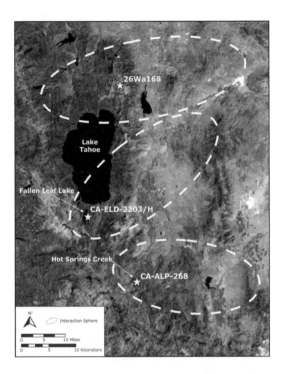

Figure 8. Local interaction spheres based on toolstone movement to the key sites.

ows and Washoe Lake are a good distance to the east, but plain to see from the high ridge. Large villages occur throughout the Truckee Meadows and are easily accessed by way of Galena Creek and down Third Creek to Ophir Creek. We believe this viewshed was essentially the core territory, what we call the local interaction sphere, of the 26Wa168 residents.

CA-ELD-2203/H

The prehistoric portion of this multicomponent site incorporates an open glade and riparian meadow surrounded by conifer forest at an elevation of 1,951 m (6,400 ft) on the northeast shore of Fallen Leaf Lake. Flaked stone artifacts cover approximately 10,800 m² along with several bedrock slicks and mortars. This residential site has a relatively low-density yet diverse artifact assemblage consisting of projectile points, bifaces, flake tools, debitage, groundstone implements, and bedrock milling features. As discussed above, CA-ELD-2203/H sits within the metamorphic zone; consequently, local metamorphic toolstone comprises a large part of the assemblage (34%, n = 85; Figure 4). Metamorphic debitage reflects an emphasis on core reduction, probably for flake tool manufacture. Only small frequencies of early and late stage biface reduction flakes indicate metamorphic bifacial tool manufacture, which suggests that metamorphic toolstone was limited to local use. It was probably transported between seasonally occupied higher elevation sites within the local interaction sphere, but transport to winter village sites in Carson Valley for use and exchange was likely infrequent. Further, exchange of metamorphic toolstone to groups occupying sites in the basalt and obsidian/CCS zones would have been uncommon.

Basalt and obsidian comprise 24% (n = 60) and 39% (n = 98) of the CA-ELD-2203/H assemblage (see Figure 4), respectively. In this case, the low frequencies of the lesser sources indicate directionality for toolstone transport and population interactions. Most of the flaked stone tools at CA-ELD-2203/H are basalt (64%, n = 9). The basalt debitage reflects an even continuum of biface reduction from early to late stage, as well as pressure flaking. It is apparent that basalt tools, in various stages of manufacture (including finished tools) were transported to the site. Only two basalt sources are represented in the assemblage, Alder Hill (86%, n = 6[1]) and Steamboat Hills (14%, n = 1) (Figure 5). The other kinds of basalt, available north of Lake Tahoe, are not present.

Alder Hill is common at Tahoe Sierra sites, so it is no surprise that it makes up the largest part of the basalt assemblage at the site. More telling is the absence of other North Lake Tahoe basalts, which suggests that CA-ELD-2203/H residents did not regularly utilize this area and may not have acquired Alder Hill toolstone directly. In addition, the low frequency of Steamboat basalt indicates that CA-ELD-2203/H populations did not have direct access to the Steamboat source. Due to its superior quality, Steamboat basalt would have been used if it was readily available. It is likely that basalt was exchanged during winters (Figure 7) when populations from across the Tahoe Sierra occupied villages in the Carson Valley (Nevers 1976:16). However, Alder Hill basalt appears to have been more accessible for a number of reasons, including its abundance at the source, its good quality, and most importantly, its central location within North Lake Tahoe geography. Near the Truckee River on the northwestern margin of Martis Valley, Alder Hill was a rich environment occupied at least seasonally by relatively large populations (Lindström 2000; McGuire et al. 2006) that would have wintered primarily east in Carson Valley and the Truckee Meadows. In addition, it is located in proximity to the trans-Sierran travel route over Donner Pass. For all these reasons, Alder Hill basalt was used most frequently as a general toolstone and was more likely to be exchanged between small groups throughout the year (Nevers 1976:20) and during larger winter gatherings. Obsidian tells a similar story. Bodie Hills accounts for 91% (n = 10; see Figure 6) of the obsidian in the CA-ELD-2203/H sample. Like Alder Hill basalt, Bodie Hills obsidian is ubiquitous and typically found at high frequencies at sites throughout the Tahoe Sierra. Obsidian exchange relied on connections with the Bodie Hills source throughout prehistory to import large quantities of this high-quality toolstone. Over time, the exchange network shifted south to increase the import frequency of Bodie Hills obsidian (Bloomer and Jaffke 2009b). In addition, and most importantly, only 9% (n = 1) of the obsidian sample from CA-ELD-2203/H is Sutro Springs obsidian. As with Steamboat Hills basalt, if Sutro Springs was more available then it should be present at higher frequencies in the CA-ELD-2203/H assemblage. Hence, Sutro Springs was probably not procured directly by site occupants. Instead, it was likely exchanged at winter villages in Carson Valley as the primary means of procurement before being transported into the high country (Figure 7).

The local interaction sphere of populations living at CA-ELD-2203/H did not incorporate North Tahoe or the Truckee Meadows on a regular basis. Rather, the South Tahoe local interaction sphere was essentially oriented from winter villages in the Carson Valley, trending southwest towards seasonal habitations and resource areas to the south (Figure 8), encompassing an area of approximately 1,200 km². The Carson Range offers low-elevation passes for access from the Carson Valley to Tahoe's eastern and southern shores. Populations in the southern Carson Valley could also travel up the West Fork of the Carson River to access Lake Tahoe, as well as the high country from Tahoe south to Carson Pass.

CA-ALP-268

Site CA-ALP-268, located at an elevation of 5,800 ft, incorporates approximately 5,600 m² on terraces above Hot Springs Creek. A 20-m diameter central activity locus is situated on a sagebrush-covered flat nestled against the lower slopes of a glacial knoll and is bounded to the south by a meadow. Bedrock milling stations with slicks and mortars are located within the central locus and on the terrace edge overlooking Hot Springs Creek. The flaked stone artifact assemblage is comprised of CCS and obsidian tools, including projectile points, bifacial tools, a drill, a uniface, flake tools, and cores, representing a variety of tool use activities. High frequencies of obsidian and CCS debitage reflect the manufacture and maintenance of both obsidian and CCS tools.

The site assemblage does not include any basalt tools and only minimal debitage. The general paucity of basalt at the site indicates that good quality basalt toolstone, accessible within the North Tahoe interaction sphere, was not readily available to the inhabitants of CA-ALP-268. Basalt exchange with northern populations apparently was limited.

Bodie Hills obsidian is highly represented at CA-ALP-268 (91%, n = 21; see Figure 6), even though the source is located 80 km southeast of the site. Mt. Hicks, located 24 km east of the Bodie Hills source, makes up the remaining 9% (n = 2) of the obsidian sample. Sutro Springs and other northern source materials are not represented in the assemblage, indicating a closer connection with the southeastern sources than the more proximal northern sources.

The CA-ALP-268 assemblage is also characterized by a high frequency of CCS tools and debitage. This is the only key site where CCS toolstone has a significant presence (Figure 4). Middle Archaic sites in the basalt and metamorphic zones typically have low CCS frequencies. Identification of CCS toolstone sources within the Tahoe Sierra is still developing, yet we know that siliceous rhyolite, a CCS toolstone in the CA-ALP-268 assemblage, may have come from fairly local sources procured in conjunction with daily resource gathering or during movement to the site (see Figure 7). Massive Pliocene volcanic flows east of the site (Koenig 1963) indicate that rhyolite was a source for small quantities of CCS toolstone (Shapiro 2010). In addition, rhyolite deposits associated with volcanic flows in the Carson Range to the north are a known source for siliceous toolstone (Lindström and Kantz 1989). Therefore, sources for CCS in the form of small siliceous rhyolite and other CCS deposits were available as local components of the volcanic geology. At the same time, and more importantly, much of the CCS at CA-ALP-268 appears to be sedimentary chert. Sources for sedimentary chert are not known within the Tahoe Sierra. Instead, the regional geology (Moore 1969) suggests that sedimentary chert was probably available as alluvial and colluvial cobbles within Quaternary deposits from 25 to 50 km east and southeast.

Taken together, the lack of basalt, the abundance of CCS, and the presence of obsidian exclusively from the southeast suggests that CA-ALP-268 residents incorporated a local interaction sphere, oriented east and southeast, an area measuring at least 1,250 km² (Figure 8). There was apparently little to no toolstone exchange from populations to the north. Bodie Hills obsidian likely moved through the local interaction spheres from south to north, but it appears that northern toolstone was not the currency of exchange to the south.

Beyond Local Interaction Spheres

The interregional Middle Archaic interaction sphere (Figure 9), previously gleaned from regional geochemical obsidian data analysis (Bloomer and Jaffke 2009b), is the larger cohesive realm within which each of the smaller local interaction spheres function. Data from each of the key sites points to the interconnectedness of each local pattern within the regional exchange network.

The movement of toolstone by way of exchange from the far reaches of an interregional network is represented primarily by the obsidian diversity at site 26Wa168 (Figure 6). Bodie Hills obsidian, from approximately 145 km southeast, accounts for 47% of the obsidian and is common at most Tahoe Sierra sites. In addition, there are low frequencies of obsidian from Mt. Hicks (8%), Queen (2%),

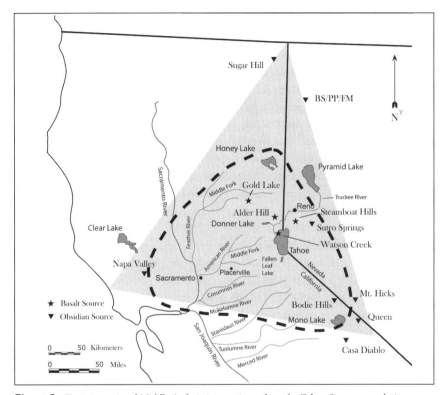

Figure 9. The interregional Middle Archaic interaction sphere for Tahoe Sierran populations is indicated by the bold dashed line. The Obsidian Triangle incorporates the far distant obsidian sources exchanged into the Tahoe Sierra. (Note: BS/PP/FM = Bordwell Spring/Pinto Peak/Fox Mountain.)

and Casa Diablo (1%), all further south and east of Bodie Hills. Small frequencies of obsidian from northern sources include Bordwell Spring/Pinto Peak/Fox Mountain (BS/PP/FM; 3%), located approximately 194 km north in northwestern Nevada, and Sugar Hill (2%), located at least 260 km away in far northeastern California (see Figure 8). In addition, Napa obsidian (2%) was transported from its source, approximately 240 km west, over the Sierran Crest. One projectile point made from Gold Lake basalt, a source located approximately 73 km northwest, suggests exchange from beyond the local interaction sphere. Gold Lake basalt accounts for only 3% of the 26Wa168 sample (Figure 5). The frequency of Gold Lake basalt is much higher at more northern sites (Day et al. 1996; Waechter and Andolina 2005) where people had direct access to the quarry.

The distribution of these distant sources approximates the general realm of Middle Archaic interaction within the Obsidian Triangle (Figure 9). The Obsidian Triangle incorporates the far distant sources from which obsidian was moved into the Tahoe Sierra. The Middle Archaic interaction sphere encompasses a trans-Sierran area of approximately 75,000 km^2 within which Middle Archaic Tahoe Sierra populations exchanged obsidian from neighboring populations and then exchanged it again between local populations. Low frequencies of the most distant toolstone are common at Middle Archaic sites within the Tahoe Sierra region, indicating procurement by exchange into the local interaction spheres. Although small frequencies of the most northerly sources (Sugar Hill and BS/PP/FM) are evident in Middle Archaic sites, obsidian distribution research has shown that the Middle Archaic interaction sphere, in general, did not extend all the way to the most northern obsidian sources. This is because the proportions of toolstone from the northern obsidian sources actually decreased from the Early Archaic to Middle Archaic, indicating a Late Holocene shift in procurement and population interaction towards the south (Bloomer and Jaffke 2009b).

The highest obsidian frequencies are typically from Bodie Hills, indicating greater access to the Bodie Hills source than to the other distant sources. Hence, it is likely that Bodie Hills populations were closely connected to Tahoe Sierra populations and that Bodie Hills obsidian was regularly exchanged between local interaction spheres. It may also have been procured directly through long-distance travel, passing through several local territories to access the quarry.

Toolstone Distributions and Ancestral Washoe Land Use

The Tahoe Sierra is the heartland of the ethnographic Washoe territory (d'Azevedo 1986:468). The larger interregional interaction sphere of Middle Archaic Tahoe Sierra populations surrounds the ethnographic Washoe territory. It is no stretch of the imagination to suggest that the Middle Archaic interaction sphere (Figure 9) represents the interregional interaction sphere of the ancestral Washoe within which toolstone, and probably other resources, were exchanged with non-Washoe populations. The local interaction spheres (Figure 8) identified from the perspective of the three key sites represent territories within the Washoe heartland where ancestral Washoe habitation sites were routinely occupied and resources were regularly acquired.

In fact, the three local interaction spheres approximate the geographically different territories of the three Washoe groups: *Welmelti* (northern), *Pauwalu* (central), and *Hungalelti* (southern) (Nevers 1976). Current ethnographic research (Penny Rucks, personal communication 2011) suggests that these three populations represented zones of most frequent social interaction, even if individuals might have moved freely from one to another, adopting the identity of their new location. The interaction spheres depicted in Figure 8 come together at the ethnographic transitions between the three groups, but do not encompass the entire geographic territories of each of the groups. For example, we do not suggest that populations of the southern interaction sphere never visited Lake Tahoe. Instead, the local interaction spheres approximate routine resource procurement and seasonally occupied territories of smaller subgroups (possibly families or family collectives) relative to each geographic group. Given the unique Lake Tahoe geography and logistics of seasonal land use throughout time, our research suggests that the three Washoe groups had Middle Archaic roots, modeled as local interaction spheres interpreted archaeologically through toolstone distribution analysis.

Conclusions

Analysis of toolstone distributions from the perspective of three Middle Archaic sites illuminates the geographic and social terrain of three relatively distinct local interaction spheres within which ancestral Washoe populations occupied sites and acquired resources. These interaction spheres are a foundation for expanding our knowledge of Middle Archaic land use patterns, comparing Late Archaic land use, and modeling economics and social dynamics within and beyond the interaction spheres.

The results of our research affirm that toolstone distribution analysis will continue to be productive for Tahoe Sierra research. Its future depends on the consistent growth of the data base. At the same time, samples must be associated with chronologically well-defined assemblages. Chronological precision will continue to be an emphasis for Sierran research. While radiocarbon/obsidian hydration pairs are woefully lacking, we have learned that large excavation exposures do yield hearth and oven features containing charcoal (Bloomer and Lindström 2006a, 2006b; Waechter and Andolina 2005). Finding charcoal-bearing features within intact distinct stratigraphy associated with flaked and ground stone assemblages will advance toolstone distribution research and the greater scope of Tahoe Sierra archaeology.

Acknowledgments

Thanks go to Penny Rucks for her insightful comments and to the anonymous reviewers for their constructive criticisms on an earlier draft of this article.

Note

One basalt sample from 26Wa168 and two basalt samples from CA-ELD-2203/H, originally identified as Alder Hill/Watson Creek, were reanalyzed by Northwest

Research Obsidian Studies Lab and reclassified as Alder Hill (Craig Skinner, personal communication 2012).

References Cited

Basgall, Mark E.
  1989   Obsidian Acquisition and Use in Prehistoric Central Eastern California: A Preliminary Assessment. In *Current Directions in California Obsidian Studies*, edited by Richard E. Hughes, pp. 111–126. Contributions of the University of California Archaeological Research Facility, No. 48, Berkeley.
Basgall, Mark E., and Kelly R. McGuire
  1988   *The Archaeology of CA-INY-30: Prehistoric Culture Change in the Southern Owens Valley, California*. Report on file at the California Department of Transportation, Sacramento.
Binford, Lewis R.
  1983   Organization and Formation Processes: Looking at Curated Technologies. In *Working at Archaeology*, pp. 269–286. Academic Press, New York.
Bloomer, William W.
  2003   *Archaeological Investigations at Ma?WI? Dime?dagadup (Hawk Pond), 26Wa168/05-19-290, Washoe County, Nevada*. Report No. TB-2002-056. Report on file at U.S. Forest Service, Lake Tahoe Basin Management Unit, South Lake Tahoe, California.
  2006   *Archaeological Test Investigations at the Fredericks Prehistoric Site, CA-ELD-2203/H (FS# 05-19-621). Tahoe-Baikal Institute, Mountain Lake Environment Center, El Dorado County, California*. Report on file at Planning Solutions, Truckee, California.
Bloomer, William W., and Denise Jaffke
  2009a   *Black Point Into Lake, CA-ELD-261/H Prehistoric Artifact Collections Analysis and Research Design, Sugar Pine Point State Park, El Dorado County, California*. Report on file at California Department of Parks and Recreation, Sierra District, Tahoma.
  2009b   A High Sierran Nexus: Hot Obsidian Data from Donner Memorial State Park. *Proceedings of the Society for California Archaeology* 21:109–115.
Bloomer, William W., and Susan Lindström
  2006a   *Archaeological Data Recovery Investigations at Donner Dam, CA-NEV-13/H, Locus F/G and Locus G, Donner Memorial State Park, Nevada County, California*. Report on file at California State Parks, Sierra District, Tahoma.
  2006b   *Archaeological Investigations at Squaw Valley, Placer County, California*. Report on file at Robert Henrichs Enterprises, Inc., Rocklin, California.
Bloomer, William W., Sharon A. Waechter, and Susan Lindström
  1997   *Basalt Quarrying on Watson Creek: An Archaeological and Ethnographic Study in the Northern Lake Tahoe Basin, Vol. 1*. Report on file at the U.S. Forest Service, Lake Tahoe Basin Management Unit, South Lake Tahoe, California.
Day, Donna A., William W. Bloomer, M. Kathleen Davis, and Thomas L. Jackson
  1996   Basalt Distribution as a Reflection of Procurement and Mobility Across the North-Central Sierra. Paper presented at the 25th Great Basin Anthropological Conference, Kings Beach, California.

d'Azevedo, Warren L.

1986   The Washoe. In *Great Basin*, edited by Warren L. d'Azevedo, pp. 466–499. *Handbook of North American Indians*, Vol.11, William G. Sturtevant, general editor. Smithsonian Institution, Washington, D.C.

Delacorte, Michael G., and Kelly R. McGuire

1993   *Archaeological Test Evaluation at Twenty-three Sites Located Along a Proposed Fiber-Optic Telephone Cable Route in Owens Valley, California.* Report on file at the Bureau of Land Management, California Desert District, Moreno Valley.

Frazetti, Daryl, and Ian Morris

2008   Site Record for Site 05-19-982. Record on file at U.S. Forest Service, Lake Tahoe Basin Management Unit, South Lake Tahoe, California.

Hughes, Richard E.

1986   Diachronic Variability in Obsidian Procurement Patterns in Northeastern California and Southcentral Oregon. *University of California Publications in Anthropology* 17, Berkeley.

1992   Northern California Obsidian Studies: Some Thoughts and Observations on the First Two Decades. *Proceedings of the Society for California Archaeology* 4:113–122.

Jackson, Robert J., Thomas L. Jackson, Charles Miksicek, Kristina Roper, and Dwight Simons

1994   *Framework for Archaeological Research and Management, National Forests of the North-Central Sierra Nevada.* Report on file at USDA Forest Service, Eldorado National Forest, California.

Jaffke, Denise, and William W. Bloomer

2008   *Archaeological Excavation Report & Evaluation for Three Prehistoric Sites: CA-ALP-117, CA-ALP-118 & CA-ALP-268, Grover Hot Springs State Park, Alpine County, California.* Report on file at California Department of Parks and Recreation, Sierra District, Tahoma.

Koenig, James B.

1963   Geologic Map of California, Walker Lake Sheet. *California Division of Mines and Geology.*

Latham, Thomas S., Paula A. Sutton, and Kenneth L. Verosub

1992   Non-Destructive XRF Characterization of Basaltic Artifacts from Truckee, California. *Geoarchaeology: An International Journal* 7(2):81–102.

Lindström, Susan G.

2000   *Heritage Resource Inventory, Planned Community-2, Boca Sierra Estates Specific Plan Project, 789 Acres near Truckee, California, Nevada County. Volume I: Report.* Report on file at Pacific Municipal Consultants, Sacramento, California.

Lindström, Susan G., and V. Kantz

1989   Site Record for Site 05-19-206. Record on file at the North Central Information Center, California State University, Sacramento.

Lindström, Susan, William W. Bloomer, Penny Rucks, and D. Craig Young

2002   *Lake Tahoe Environmental Improvement Program Restoration and Rehabilitation of Truckee River Outlet Parcel: Volume 1, Contextual Background.* Report on file at California Department of Parks and Recreation, Sacramento.

Maher, John, and Karen Blom

1999   Site Record for Site 05-19-943. Record on file at U.S. Forest Service, Lake Tahoe Basin Management Unit, South Lake Tahoe, California.

Markley, Richard E., and Donna A. Day

1992   Regional Prehistory and California-Great Basin Interaction: An Assessment of Recent Archaeological Studies in the Northern Sierra Nevada. *Proceedings of the Society for California Archaeology* 4:171–192.

Martin, Thomas P.
    1998   Archaeological Test Excavations at the Visitor Center Site: An Early Holocene Site in Lake
            Tahoe, California. Unpublished Master's thesis, Sonoma State University, Rohnert Park,
            California.
McGuire, Kelly R., and William W. Bloomer
    1997   Middle Period Land-Use Patterns and Toolstone Preferences: A Model for the Martis
            Complex and Other North-Central Sierran and Eastern Front Assemblages. In *Culture
            Change Along the Eastern Sierra Nevada/Cascade Front: Volume VI, Fort Sage Uplands and
            Spanish Springs Valley*, by Kelly R. McGuire, pp. 115–122. Report on file at Tuscarora Gas
            Transmission Company, Reno, Nevada.
McGuire, Kelly R., Sharon A. Waechter, D. Craig Young, and Daron Duke
    2006   *Archaeological Investigations at the Alder Hill Prehistoric Basalt Quarry, Nevada County:
            Volume I, Prehistoric Sites*. Report on file at East West Partners, Truckee, California.
Moore, James G.
    1969   Geologic Map of Lyon, Douglas, and Ormsby Counties, Nevada. In *Geology and Mineral
            Deposits of Lyon, Douglas, and Ormsby Counties, Nevada*. Nevada Bureau of Mines and Geol-
            ogy Bulletin 75. University of Nevada, Reno.
Nevers, Jo Ann
    1976   *WA SHE SHU: A Washo Tribal History.* Inter-Tribal Council of Nevada, Reno.
Rosenthal, Jeffrey, and Jack Meyer
    2011   Development of an Empirically Based Hydration Rate for Bodie Hills Obsidian. In *A New
            Frame of Reference: Prehistoric Cultural Chronology and Ecology in the North-Central Sierra
            Nevada*, edited by Jeffrey Rosenthal, pp. 7–15. Center for Archaeological Research at
            Davis, Publication No. 16.
Saucedo, George J.
    2005   Geologic Map of the Lake Tahoe Basin, California and Nevada. *California Geological Survey,
            Regional Geologic Map Series No. 4.*
Saucedo, George J., and D. L. Wagner
    1992   Geologic Map of the Chico Quadrangle, California. *California Division of Mines and Geology,
            Regional Geologic Map Series No. 7A.*
Shapiro, Lisa
    2010   *Class III Cultural Resources Inventory in Alpine County, California*. Bureau of Land Manage-
            ment Report No. CCR3-2406. Report on file at U.S. Department of the Interior, Bureau of
            Land Management, Carson City Field Office, Nevada.
Skinner, Craig E., and M. Kathleen Davis
    1996   *X-Ray Fluorescence Analysis of Artifact Basalt from the Tahoe and Eldorado National Forests,
            California: The Oakland Pond Project*. Report on file at Tahoe National Forest, Nevada City,
            California.
Waechter, Sharon A., and Darren Andolina
    2005   *Ecology and Prehistory in Sierra Valley, California: Excavations at CA-PLU-1485*. Report on
            file at California Department of Transportation, District 2, Redding.
Wagner, D. L., C. W. Jennings, T. L. Bedrossian, and E. J. Bortugno
    1981   *Geologic Map of the Sacramento Quadrangle, California*. California Division of Mines and
            Geology, Regional Geologic Map Series No. 1A.

REPORT

A Fluted Projectile Point from Crystal Cove State Park, Orange County, Alta California

Richard T. Fitzgerald
California State Parks, Archaeology History and Museums Division,
2505 Port Street, West Sacramento, CA 95691 (rfitzgerald@parks.ca.gov)

Michael F. Rondeau
Rondeau Archeological, 251 Rockmont Circle, Sacramento, CA 95835
(mikerondo@yahoo.com)

Abstract   Fluted projectile points are rarely found along the California coast. Only three have been previously documented, one from northern California and two from southern California. A fourth found in Orange County is reported here. This isolated artifact made of local material suggests a Clovis presence along the California littoral at the end of the Pleistocene. We re-examine the evidence of Clovis in California in light of the early occupation of Santarosae Island and explore the possible relationship between Clovis and the Late Pleistocene occupation of the Santa Barbara Channel Islands.

Resumen   Rara vez se encuentran puntas acanaladas de proyectil en la costa de California. Se han documentado antes sólo tres puntas: uno en el norte de California, y dos en el sur de California. Se informe aquí de una cuarta, encontrada en el Condado de Orange. Este artefacto aislado, hecho de material local, sugiere una presencia Clovis a lo largo de la litoral californiana al final del Pleistoceno. Volvimos a examinar las pruebas de Clovis en California a la luz de la ocupación temprana de la isla de Santarosae y investigamos la relación posible entre Clovis y la ocupación de las Islas Canal de Santa Bárbara en el Pleistoceno tardío.

Although hundreds of fluted projectile points have been reported from within California (e.g., Dillon 2002; Hopkins 1991; Mills et al. 2005; Moratto et al. 2011; Riddell and Olsen 1969; Rondeau 2006), only a handful has been discovered

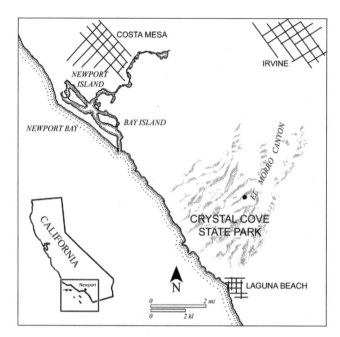

Figure 1. Location of Crystal Cove State Park and El Morro Canyon.

along the coast. The general dearth of fluted points found along the Pacific shore has had a major influence on the models of the initial colonization of western North America (e.g., Beck and Jones 2010; Erlandson et al. 2007; Fladmark 1979). As such, each individual find of a fluted point near the coastline has significance. Previously, only three fluted points have been documented within sight of the California littoral: one from Mendocino County (Simons et al. 1985), one from Santa Barbara County (Erlandson et al. 1987), and one from Los Angeles County (Stickel 2000). A fourth and the first ever from Orange County, the "El Morro" point, is reported here. This point is named for its location within El Morro Canyon in what is now Crystal Cove State Park (Figures 1 and 2).

Discovery of the Artifact

Credit for discovery of the point goes to Ron Sizemore, a local resident who found the artifact in 1982 while hiking in the San Joaquin Hills, which overlook the Pacific Ocean in southwestern Orange County. The point was lying on the surface of a firebreak road and likely had been unearthed during construction of the road bed. The firebreak road passes just meters from a natural spring located at 182 m amsl, just below the break-in-slope of a northwest-southeast trending ridge. The

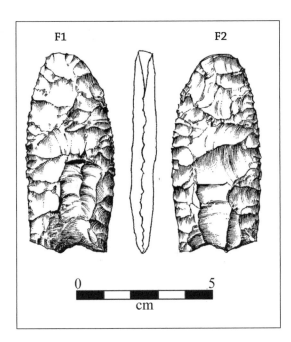

Figure 2. Fluted projectile point from Crystal Cove State Park. Illustrated by Rusty Van Rossmann.

spring forms the head of El Morro Canyon watershed, which trends southwest 4.7 km to the present ocean shore. The ridge directly above the spring offers an unobstructed view of the Pacific Ocean. From this vantage point, Santa Catalina Island, situated approximately 53 kilometers offshore, can be seen on clear days. During Clovis times, the coastline was not much further out from its present location (3 km or less) owing to the steepness of the continental shelf along this portion of the California coast (Masters and Aiello 2007).

Description

The following descriptions are made in reference to either Face 1 (F1) or Face 2 (F2) of the artifact. Descriptions referencing locations to the left or right on either face are made with the distal end oriented to the top of the page. The El Morro point is made from mottled reddish-brown and white cryptocrystalline silicate material readily identifiable as Monterey chert. It is only the fifth fluted point confirmed to be of Monterey chert in California.

The artifact measures 72.15 mm long, 33.41 mm wide, and 9 mm thick. It weighs 26.8 g. The distal end is fire-reddened where the right lateral margin (F1 view) has been lost due to a thermally induced fracture. The basal margin is missing due to at least two different damage events. The distal end of the point scar on F1 shows two percussion scar remnants, one from each margin. At a minimum these are overface flake scars if not overshot scars. The blade element of F2 shows remnants of three percussion overface flake scars that might also have been overshots. The most proximal of the three is overlapped by the termination of the flute scar. The left (F1 view) diagonal corner break is a post-burning bending fracture. The concave right portion of the damaged proximal margin (F1 view) shows some weathering under magnification that occurred prior to the burning event. This includes both the margin damage from F2 that created the off-center concavity as well as the damage scar from the lower right (F1 view) lateral margin of the base.

The point has small-to medium-sized pressure flakes indicative of edge retouching along both margins of both faces for the basal and blade segments. Under low magnification, edge grinding is apparent on both lateral margins with a trace of striations that run parallel to the biface edges. The blade element appears to have been resharpened. The proximal portions of the flutes on both faces diverge from each other when viewed in long section. The distal segments of both flutes run parallel to each other. The interior of the blade element on both faces shows remnants of soft hammer percussion scars. Due to the proximal margin damage, it is unknown if the base was concave or if there was basal grinding.

Unlike many fluted points from California, this specimen is notably large and thick in cross section. These attributes, along with the length of the flutes and lateral margin grinding and overface/overshot flake scars on the blade element, lend support to the classification of this point as a "true" Clovis point and not a Far West fluted variant that typically are thinner, more gracile, and presumably younger than Clovis (Rondeau et al. 2007). If indeed this is a genuine Clovis point (i.e., attributable to the Clovis culture), it is plausible that it dates to the Late Pleistocene, or ca. 11,050 to 10,800 RCYBP (Waters and Stafford 2007).

Discussion

Historically, California has never attracted much attention when the Clovis culture is debated and has therefore had a diminished role in models pertaining to the initial settlement of North America (e.g., Beck and Jones 2012; Erlandson 2002; Erlandson et al. 2007, 2011; Fiedel and Morrow 2012). For example, in Waters and Stafford's (2007) synthesis on the age of Clovis (where they re-dated 11 key sites), not a single mention was made of Clovis sites in California (the only California site mentioned at all was the Arlington Springs human remains from Santa Rosa Island [Johnson et al. 2000]).

There are at least two sites in cismontane California that have produced numerous fluted points: the Borax Lake Site (CA-LAK-36) in the Clear Lake Basin (Harrington 1948) and the Witt site (CA-KIN-32) at Tulare Lake (Riddell and Olsen 1969) in the southern Central Valley. Unfortunately, each has proven difficult to precisely date. The Witt site is predominately a surface scatter along the margins of Tulare Lake, and the Borax Lake site has a highly mixed Paleoindian deposit and later archaeological components (Meighan and Haynes 1970).

Beyond these two sites, there is a wide distribution of isolated fluted points throughout California representing every environmental setting in the state, including the high and low deserts (Basgall 1988; Campbell and Campbell 1935; Davis et al. 1980), the Sierra Nevada (Foster and Betts 1995; Moratto et al. 2011) and their foothills (La Jeunesse and Pryor 1996), the North Coast Ranges (Dillon 2002), the Central Coast Ranges (Bertrando 2004; Mills et al. 2005) and the Central Valley (Fenenga 1992; Wallace and Riddell 1991). Despite this geographical distribution, we have no direct economic evidence from Clovis-age sites anywhere in California (Rosenthal and Fitzgerald 2012). No "signature" mammoth or any other Pleistocene mammal kill site has yet been found in California. Yet, if Waters and Stafford (2007:1124) are correct about the timing and "rapid spread of Clovis technology" across North America between 13, 250 and 12,800 calendar years B.P. (a span of some 450 years), then the El Morro specimen and other coastal fluted points may be part of that expansion.

The question of Clovis points on the California coast is what to make of them in light of a clear human presence on the northern Santa Barbara Channel Islands at the end of the Pleistocene. In addition to the aforementioned Arlington Springs remains dated to ca. 12,900 cal B.P. (Johnson et al. 2000) on Santa Rosa Island, there are several new radiocarbon dates from Santa Rosa and San Miguel islands that range between 10,800 and 10,950 RCYBP or 11,995 to 12,920 cal B.P. (Erlandson et al. 2011). These dates are associated with what Erlandson et al. (2011:1184) called Channel Island Barb points (CIB), along with eccentric and lunate crescents, biface preforms, abundant debitage, and abraded bone tools that they argue provide evidence for a "Terminal Pleistocene seafaring, island colonization." The CIB points are stemmed, made from local island cherts, and "are of various sizes and shapes, some with elongated stems and pronounced barbs, others with shorter stems or barbs and serrated blade margins" (Erlandson et al. 2011:1184). The earliest date for these points is 12,200 cal B.P. (Erlandson et al. 2011).

Thus, beyond the Arlington Springs remains, there is only one new radiocarbon date that is of Clovis age (10,900 ± 45 RCYBP from CA-SMI-679E) and it is the least secure date in terms of its cultural origins (Erlandson et al. 2011:1184). This minimum temporal overlap, combined with the lack of an assemblage with the Arlington remains, leaves open the possibility that Clovis hunters made it out to Santarosae Island and then retreated to the mainland "using simple watercraft"

(Fiedel and Morrow 2012:380). There are, however, two lines of evidence that make this scenario highly unlikely. First, as Beck and Jones (2012) pointed out, no fluted points have ever been found on any of the Santa Barbara Channel Islands. Second, the assemblage of thin, delicately barbed CIB points, although as much as 600 years younger than the presumed age of Clovis, seems to be so technologically divergent from Clovis lithic technology that it seems improbable they are related from a cultural historical perspective.

What the locations of the El Morro artifact and the three other isolated fluted points found along the California coast strongly suggest is that their Clovis makers were well aware of the coast and its resources, evident by their use of locally available Monterey chert to fashion these artifacts. Fluted points discovered throughout California and made from a variety of materials—including all of the major obsidian sources from east to west of the Sierra Nevada (e.g., Borax Lake, Casa Diablo, Coso, Napa Glass Mountain) as well as high-quality cryptocrystalline silicates (i.e., Franciscan and Monterey chert)—bear witness to the makers' intimate familiarity with the economic geology of California. They also suggest that the region was already widely explored by about 13,000 years ago (Rosenthal and Fitzgerald 2012).

Intriguing obsidian hydration data generated from a large obsidian quarry and sites in the southeast region of the state (Basgall 1988; Basgall and Hall 1991; Gilreath and Hildebrandt 1997) provide a rough age estimate for a Clovis presence in the high deserts of California. But without absolute dates on large fluted points, such as the El Morro specimen, the questions remain: (1) how old are such points on the coast, and (2) if they date to the terminal Pleistocene, were their makers the first to reach the continent's edge?

Acknowledgments

The authors wish to thank Mr. Sizemore for allowing us to study this important find, which included having it drawn, photographed, and generally passed around for an extended period of time. We also thank Rusty Van Rossmann for his maps and the quick turnaround time. We thank the editor and reviewers for their constructive comments and lastly we wish to thank Candice Ralston with assistance on the references cited section.

References Cited

Basgall, Mark E.
  1988   Archaeology of the Komodo Site, An Early Holocene Occupation in Central-Eastern California (The Archaeology of CA-MNO-679: a Pre-Archaic Site in Long Valley Caldera, Mono County, California). In *Early Human Occupation in Far Western North America: The*

Clovis Archaic Interface, edited by Judith A. Willig, C. Melvin Akins, and John L. Fagan, pp. 103–119. Nevada State Museum Anthropological Papers No. 21.

Basgall, Mark E., and Matt C. Hall
    1991   Relationships Between Fluted and Stemmed Points in the Mojave Desert. *Current Research in the Pleistocene.* 8:61–64.

Beck, Charlotte, and George T. Jones
    2010   Clovis and Western Stemmed: Population Migration and the Meeting of Two Technologies in the Intermountain West. *American Antiquity* 75:81–116.
    2012   Clovis and Western Stemmed Again: Reply to Fiedel and Morrow. *American Antiquity* 77:386–397.

Bertrando, Ethan B.
    2004   Evidence and Models for Late Pleistocene Chronology and Settlement Along California's Central Coast. In *Emerging from the Ice Age: Early Holocene Occupations on the California Central Coast,* edited by Ethan Bertrando and Valerie A. Levulett, pp. 93–105. San Luis Obispo County Archaeological Society Occasional Papers No. 17.

Campbell, Elizabeth C., and William H. Campbell
    1935   *The Pinto Basin Site: An Ancient Aboriginal Camping Ground in the California Desert.* Southwest Museum Papers No. 9. Los Angeles.

Davis, Emma L., Kathryn H. Brown, and Jacqueline Nichols
    1980   *Evaluation of Early Human Activities and Remains in the California Desert.* Bureau of Land Management, Cultural Resources Publications, Anthropology-History, Barstow.

Dillon, Brian D.
    2002   California Paleoindians: Lack of Evidence, or Evidence of Lack? In *Essays in California Archaeology, A Memorial to Franklin Fenenga,* edited by William J. Wallace and Frances A. Riddell, pp. 110–128. Contributions of the University of California Archaeological Research Facility 60.

Erlandson, Jon M.
    2002   Anatomically Modern Humans, Maritime Voyaging, and the Pleistocene Colonization of the Americas. In *The First Americans: The Pleistocene Colonization of the New World,* edited by Nina G. Jablonski, pp. 59–92. Memoirs of the California Academy of Sciences No. 27.

Erlandson, Jon M., Theodore G. Cooley, and Richard Carrico
    1987   A Fluted Projectile Point Fragment from the Southern California Coast: Chronology and Context at CA-SBA-1951. *Journal of California and Great Basin Anthropology* 9:120–128.

Erlandson, Jon M., Torben C. Rick, Terry L. Jones, and Judith F. Porcasi
    2007   One If by Land, Two If by Sea: Who Were the First Californians? In *California Prehistory: Colonization, Culture, and Complexity,* edited by Terry L. Jones and Kathryn A. Klar, pp. 53–62. AltaMira Press, Lanham, Maryland.

Erlandson, Jon M., Torben C. Rick, Todd J. Braje, Molly Casperson, Brendan Culleton, Brian Fulfrost, Tracy Garcia, Daniel A. Guthrie, Nicholas Jew, Douglas J. Kennett, Madonna L. Moss, Leslie Reeder, Craig Skinner, Jack Watts, and Lauren Willis
    2001   Paleoindian Seafaring, Maritime Technologies, and Coastal Foraging on California's Channel Islands. *Science* 331:1181–1184.

Fenenga, Gerrit L.
    1992   Regional Variability in the Early Prehistory of the American Far West. Ph.D. dissertation, Department of Anthropology, University of California, Berkeley. Manuscript on file, University Microfilms, Ann Arbor.

Fiedel, Stuart J., and Juliet E. Morrow

2012   Comment on "Clovis and Western Stemmed: Population Migration and the Meetings of
         Two Technologies in the Intermountain West" by Charlotte Beck and George T. Jones.
         American Antiquity 77:376–385.

Fladmark, Knut R.

1979   Routes: Alternate Migration Corridors for Early Man in North America. *American Antiq-
         uity* 44:55–69.

Foster, Dan, and John Betts

1995   A Fluted Point from Sierra Valley. *Tulare Lake Archaeological Research Group Report* 8:304.

Gilreath, Amy J., and William R. Hildebrandt

1997   *Prehistoric Use of the Coso Volcanic Field.* Contributions of the University of California
         Archaeological Research Facility No. 56.

Harrington, Mark R.

1948   *An Ancient Site at Borax Lake, California.* Southwest Museum Papers No. 16. Los Angeles.

Hopkins, Jerry

1991   Tulare Lake Fluted Points. In *Contributions to Tulare Lake Archaeology I: Background to a
         Study of Tulare Lake's Archaeological Past,* edited by William J. Wallace and Francis A. Rid-
         dell, pp. 34–40. Tulare Lake Archaeological Research Group, Redondo Beach.

Johnson, John R., Thomas W. Stafford, Jr., Henry O. Ajie, and Don P. Morris

2000   Arlington Springs Revisited. In *Proceedings of the Fifth California Islands Symposium,* 2 vols.,
         edited by David R. Browne, Kathryn L. Mitchell, and Henry W. Chaney, pp. 541–545.
         Santa Barbara Museum of Natural History, Santa Barbara.

LaJeunesse, Roger M., and John M. Pryor

1996   *Skyrocket Appendices.* Report on file at the Department of Anthropology, California State
         University, Fresno.

Masters, Patricia M., and Ivano W. Aiello

2007   Postglacial Evolution of Coastal Environments. In *California Prehistory: Colonization,
         Culture, and Complexity,* edited by Terry L. Jones and Kathryn A. Klar, pp. 35–53. AltaMira
         Press, Lanham, Maryland.

Meighan, Clement, and C. Vance Haynes

1970   The Borax Lake Site Revisited. *Science* 167:1213–1221.

Mills, Wayne W., Michael F. Rondeau, and Terry L. Jones

2005   A Fluted Point from Nipomo, San Luis Obispo County, California. *Journal of California and
         Great Basin Anthropology* 25:214–220.

Moratto, Michael J., Shelly Davis-King, Jeffrey Rosenthal, and Laurie Sylwester

2011   A Second Fluted Point from Twain Harte, Central Sierra Nevada, California. *California
         Archaeology* 3:307–313.

Riddell, Francis A, and William H. Olsen

1969   An Early Man Site in the San Joaquin Valley, California. *American Antiquity* 34:121–130.

Rondeau, Michael F.

2006   Revising the Number of Reported Clovis Points from Tulare Lake, California. *Current
         Research in the Pleistocene* 23:140–142.

Rondeau, Michael F., Jim Cassidy, and Terry L. Jones
   2007   Colonization Technologies: Fluted Projectile Points and the San Clemente Island Wood-working/Microblade Complex. In *California Prehistory: Colonization, Culture, and Complexity,* edited by Terry L. Jones and Kathryn A. Klar, pp 63–70. AltaMira Press, Lanham, Maryland.

Rosenthal, Jeffrey S., and Richard T. Fitzgerald
   2011   The Paleo-Archaic Transition in Western California. In *From the Pleistocene to the Holocene: Human Organization and Cultural Transformations in Prehistoric North America,* edited by C. Britt Bousman and Bradley J. Vierra, pp. 67–103. Texas A & M University Press, College Station.

Simons, Dwight D., Thomas N. Layton, and Ruthann Knudson
   1985   A Fluted Point from the Mendocino County Coast. *Journal of California and Great Basin Anthropology* 7:260–269.

Stickle, E. Gary
   2000   *A Phase 3 Excavation and Mitigation Report on the Archaeological Site CA-Lan-451, City of Malibu, California.* Environmental Research Archaeologists–A Scientific Consortium. Prepared for Timber Rock Properties, Santa Monica.

Wallace, William J., and Frances A. Riddell (editors)
   1991   *Contributions to Tulare Lake Archaeology I: Background to a Study of Tulare Lake's Archaeological Past.* Tulare Lake Archaeological Research Group, Redondo Beach.

Waters, Michael R., and Thomas W. Stafford Jr.
   2007   Redefining the Age of Clovis: Implications for the Peopling of the Americas. *Science* 315:1122–1126.

REVIEWS

California Indian Languages
Victor Golla

2011. University of California Press, Berkeley, Los Angeles, London. xi + 380 pp. $90.00 (cloth). ISBN 978-0-520-26667-4

Reviewed by Kathryn A. Klar, University of California, Berkeley

It has been decades since I pulled my copy of John Wesley Powell's *Indian Linguistic Families of America North of Mexico* (1891) from the far left end of my shelf of books on California native languages. Though no linguist, Powell recognized the linguistic diversity of America, and when he established the Bureau of American Ethnology in 1879, documenting it was a priority, bringing together the extant manuscript miscellany of earlier observers' notes and instituting a new project of field collection. "The task involved in the ... classification," Powell (1891:215) wrote, "has been accomplished by intermittent labors extending through more than twenty years of time. The author does not desire that his work shall be considered final, but rather as initiatory and tentative. The task of studying many hundreds of languages and deriving therefrom ultimate conclusions as contributions to the science of philology is one of great magnitude, and in its accomplishment an army of scholars must be employed." Powell proposed 58 language stocks which, if distributed in equal allotments across the continent, would show a marvelous diversity but would not be particularly surprising in the world context. However, the accompanying map showed how variably sized were the territories assigned to Powell's units. Huge swathes of America were occupied by groups speaking languages clearly related to another—Algonkian, Athabascan, Shoshonean, Siouan, Muskogean, and so on. The west coast, however, from Vancouver to Baja California, is a pastel patchwork stitched to the edge of the continent. In California alone, some 23—almost exactly 40%--of Powell's 58 stocks are represented.

I began this review with Powell's prescient and landmark 1891 work because the book under review, Victor Golla's magisterial *California Indian Languages* is the fulfillment, for the California patchwork, of Powell's vision. California is one of the world's most complex classificatory challenges. It has taken the research of "an army of scholars" to make this book, but it is one man—working for twice as long as Powell—who has brought it all together into a once-in-a-hundred year work which is not only scholarly, well-footnoted, well-referenced, and bibliographically complete. It is also readable and enjoyable, and goes well beyond the 19th century ideal of merely discerning "genetic" (metaphorical) relationships.

The book is in five parts, each of which could be a monograph or book on its own, but all of which are perfectly integrated in this one text. Archaeologists will find Parts One and Five of the most practical interest. In Part One, "Introduction: Defining California as a Sociolinguistic Area," Golla sets out his conceptual framework. Languages are not disembodied entities floating free in space and time, but are anchored in communities, and small ones at that in California. Golla accepts California as a "linguistic area" and Kroeber's "tribelet" as best characterizing these communities, and points out right up front that "the most important of the defining features of the California language area was not linguistic but sociopolitical." He continues, "More precisely, it was the absence of a congruence between the linguistic and the sociopolitical." (Golla: 2) The implications of this for archaeological work are clear: We cannot make the *a priori* assumption that groups and peoples who share material culture or genetic signatures spoke the same language (or languages, since multilingualism existed to a greater or lesser extent in different communities). Both areas working together can tease out a good deal more about prehistory than either on its own. In Part Five, "Linguistic Prehistory," Golla applies this principle, and gives us the nuanced result of his encyclopedic knowledge of and lifetime of thinking about the relationship between the work of archaeologists and linguists. "Readers of this section must take into account that I am more adventuresome than some of my colleagues in entertaining what seem to me plausible speculations about Hokan and Penutian....and about the overall expansion and interinfluence of the phylum-level groups in the deep prehistory of the region." (Golla: 239) It is worth noting the Golla scrupulously avoids DNA studies. This reviewer suspects that this is because molecular biology as a method for studying prehistory is still in an early state of development, much as linguistics and archaeology were prior to Boasian professionalisation. Methodologically sexy as it is, it is too soon to know exactly what DNA is telling us about California prehistory, but it isn't telling us what language someone spoke.

Part Two, "History of Study," is a chronological account of the "army of scholars" who have collected and analyzed the material on which this book is based. As one reads, considering how American linguistics developed side by side with American archaeology promises many hours of enjoyable intellection. Part Three, "Languages and Language Families," goes far beyond updating Powell. Golla does say that "[m]ore than a century after its publication, most of [Powell's 58 stock] classificatory scheme remains intact, although many of Powell's language family names...have long been abandoned." (Golla: 35) One of the real accomplishments of this book is Golla's synthesis of a mass of data which probably dwarfs anything Powell could have imagined. The most technically "linguistic" portion of the book is Part Four, "Typological and Areal Features." It is also one that will reward archaeologists who give it attention with a number of ideas about how linguistics can help inform archaeological interpretation. A prime example (but only one of many) is the plethora of counting systems in California, and the widespread lexical borrowing in this domain. This must be related to trade relations among different groups at different times and places; sorting it out will require the joint attention of both linguists and archaeologists.

Powell's study sits at the left end of my bookshelf. This volume will hold the space at the right end of the same shelf, bookending two landmarks in the study of native Californian languages. But I doubt that will happen for a long while. I plan to read and reread, noting challenges and testing hypotheses that Golla presents, for as long as I can imagine into the future. When the time comes to shelve it, I expect it will look much as does my copy of Powell, purchased in 1969. The binding will be a bit shaky, the spine creased, the pages well-thumbed and marked. And that's as it should be, for this is a book to be used, not just admired.

Reference

J. W. Powell

   1891   *Indian Linguistic Families of America North of Mexico*. University of Nebraska Press, Lincoln.

REVIEWS

Grave Matters: Excavating California's Buried Past
Tony Platt

2011. Heyday. xv + 237 pp. $18.95 (paper), ISBN 978-1-59714-162-8

Reviewed by Tsim D. Schneider, Pacific Legacy, Inc.

Most archaeologists are familiar with the participation of a Native American monitor, or community, in an archaeological project. This practice, whether legally mandated or personally cultivated, is the result of making archaeology accessible—and holding archaeologists accountable—to indigenous communities affected by our work. This was not always the case in California, where archaeology and collecting for museums have deep, intertwined, and troubled pasts. *Grave Matters: Excavating California's Buried Past* explores this past and also touches on themes of repatriation, site preservation, and community-based archaeology. This book targets a broad audience and is relevant to many interested members of the public, including Native Americans, archaeologists, museum specialists, and students.

The opening chapter frames the text's overarching theme, namely complicating the "rosy-hued story of northern California" (p. 4) by juxtaposing "the grandeur of the region's scenery with its killing fields" (p. 4). A description of the funeral for the author's son at Big Lagoon provides a comparative base from which Platt explores the connections California Indians have to ancestral places. The author addresses how these connections are marginalized or, more often, forgotten in popular memory. In northwestern California, as in much of the state, Euroamerican colonization, epidemic diseases, displacement, and the destruction and plundering of sites have crippled how Indians maintain connections to sites and to deceased relatives buried within.

These linkages are presented in Chapter 2, which orients the reader to the rich physical and cultural background of California's northwest coast. The past, Platt writes, "never rests in peace; it is always in motion, subject to revision and reinterpretation" (p. 27). The job of (re)interpreting the pasts of California Indians has historically belonged to anthropologists. Thus, Chapter 3 examines the work Alfred Kroeber and his colleagues who either collected and preserved cultural information from "uncontaminated" California tribes or, conversely, sealed the fate of Indian communities believed to be culturally or physically extinct. Students and scholars will find Platt's summary of the salvage ethnography program easy to follow, and many will find the integration of departmental correspondences insightful.

The next three chapters address reasons for the supposed "disappearance" of Indians; they detail the grim impact of routine massacres, bounty hunting, and

California Archaeology, Volume 4, Number 2, December 2012, pp. 260–262.

infectious disease on Indian communities. As Platt also explains in Chapter 5, California was part of a domestic and international collecting enterprise in which locals and academics often collaborated in the excavation, trade, and sale of artifacts and human remains to museums and anthropology departments. The "collecting bug" (p. 76) in northwestern California lead to the destruction of countless Indian villages and cemeteries for profit or study.

Despite the tandem impacts of colonialism and the desecration of ancestral sites in California, as early as 1847 "vigorous complaint" (p. 123) over the destruction of graves and villages emerged from Indians and non-Indians alike. While many readers will be familiar with the Red Power Movement of the 1960s and 1970s, Chapter 7 examines the formation of grassroots organizations (e.g., Northwest Indian Cemetery Protection Association) that sought to protect Indian graves and villages in northwestern California. Confrontation over archaeological excavations at Tsurai and Tsahpekw are showcased. Chapter 8 covers: key state and national laws that now protect Indian graves and cultural resources; the adoption of ethical research standards for archaeologists; and the repatriation process.

Punctuated with searing prose, *Grave Matters* draws attention to the fragility of cultural resources in California and to joint-California Indian and non-native efforts to stop the destruction of Indian graves and village sites. Moreover, Chapters 8 and 9 expand on the damaging effects of "airbrushing" (p. 177) the past and the great potential for museums to confront and memorialize the past "in all its troubling discomfort" (p. 183). *Grave Matters* is especially timely in California, for its discussion of collaborative partnerships between Indians and archaeologists and for reflecting on the continued importance of productive dialogues between them. Sustained budget cuts and State Park closures may lead to an increase in looting and the desecration of graves. Indeed, "the Skull Wars, alas, seem far from over" (Thomas 2000:276).

As *Grave Matters* reminds us, public awareness concerning California's dark past and finite cultural resources is a job for archaeologists, historians, writers, and native peoples alike. Yet, without diminishing the real and lasting legacies of colonialism that continue to reverberate within California Indian communities, we should also be looking beyond entrenched narratives of indigenous demise and marginality. Platt's point concerning public commemoration and the necessity for educational places that showcase "reflection, storytelling, histories, and rituals" (p. 183) is well taken. And while I agree that death most certainly "changes the meaning of a place" (p. 4), the author's overemphasis of death, monuments to Indian "genocide," and cemeteries "for the burial, symbolic and actual, of the unclaimed dead" (p. 182) may only reinforce themes of indigenous decline.

The book is accessible and well written, although the choice of photographs, especially sensitive images of village locations and the human remains appearing in Chapter 6, could have benefited from a critical review prior to their publication. In all, *Grave Matters* summarizes important developments at the busy and well-travelled intersection of California archaeology and California Indian history. The book speaks to the importance of understanding these developments and their relevance to all segments of society, and it also reminds us of the critical conversations about excavation, curation, site preservation, and repatriation that still need to take place.

Reference

Thomas, David Hurst
  2000   *Skull Wars: Kennewick Man, Archaeology, and the Battle for Native American Identity*. Basic Books, New York.

REVIEWS

An Archaeological Perspective on the Human History of Red Rock Canyon State Park: The Results of Site Survey Work 1986–2006
Michael P. Sampson

2010. California Department of Parks and Recreation Archaeology, History and Museum Division Publications in Cultural Heritage, No. 27. viii+104 pp. $12.00 (paper)

Reviewed by Mark W. Allen, California State Polytechnic University, Pomona

Red Rock Canyon is one of the most striking landscapes in the western Mojave Desert. First time visitors are often surprised by the sudden appearance of colorful Miocene age volcanic tuff formations as the highway descends into the canyon. They are also frequently struck by the familiarity of the place as most travelers through the canyon have already seen it in movies and television programs—it has been a favorite location to film Westerns and science fiction as far back as the 1920s. As Mark Faull (2004) has pointed out, Hollywood's long use of the canyon has had a world-wide impact on the perception of the American West. Red Rock Canyon was designated a California State Park in the late 1960s, and had its size dramatically increased by the California Desert Act of 1994 which transferred the Last Chance Canyon parcel from the Bureau of Land Management. Besides the dramatic geological scenery, Red Rock Canyon preserves a rich set of cultural resources.

This monograph is an addition to the Publications in Cultural Heritage series from the Archaeology, History and Museums Division of the California Department of Parks and Recreation. The author, Michael P. Sampson, presents a summary of archaeological investigations conducted over two decades (1986-2006) at Red Rock Canyon State Park. Most of this work was undertaken by the author and other California State Parks staff, especially Mark Faull who worked in the park for many years. Significant research was also conducted by faculty and students from California State University, Bakersfield. The volume also presents recommendations for the management of the park's cultural and geological resources, including opportunities for educating the public. While management concerns are often emphasized over data or other research findings, the monograph effectively demonstrates the wealth of cultural resources protected by the park, and it will be of considerable use to regional specialists.

The publication contains four main sections. The first provides an overview of the park that includes administrative history, environmental setting, background on the Kawaiisu, summaries of regional prehistory and history, and a history of archaeological investigations conducted at Red Rock Canyon. The second section details individual projects conducted in the park between 1986 and 2006. The

California Archaeology, Volume 4, Number 2, December 2012, pp. 263–265.

263

third section comprises the majority of the volume as it summarizes the results of fieldwork and archival research. This includes a total of 123 prehistoric sites, 45 historic sites, and 52 isolated finds. The summary is organized by geographic areas within the park.

The last section of the monograph presents some summary observations of interest to regional specialists. First, the majority of the prehistoric sites in the park date to the Gypsum and Rose Spring Periods, or from roughly 4000 to 850 BP. One key point made, however, is that there are significant lithic quarries located on gravel pavements in the southwestern part of the park which evidently date to the Early or Middle Holocene. These focused primarily on igneous and quartzite material. Previous research in the central Mojave has shown a distinct preference for basalt and other igneous material by tool makers during the Lake Mohave and Pinto Complexes, followed by a shift to chert and other siliceous material in later periods. This pattern holds for Red Rock Canyon as well-- by the start of the Gypsum Complex quarry activity evidently shifted to chert deposits in the north end of the park. This appears to have been a direct procurement strategy with small camps established adjacent to quarries, as well as evidence that material was heat-treated on site, and reduced to biface blanks for transportation to other areas. For the historical period, Sampson stresses the significance of the numerous mining sites which date between the 1890s to the latter part of the 20th century. Particularly important are well-preserved dry placer mining landscapes as these are relatively rare worldwide. He further notes that cultural resources and landscapes associated with 19th and 20th century transportation, construction of the Los Angeles Aqueduct, tourism, and the film industry are also key components of Red Rock Canyon.

Another point made in the concluding section is that Red Rock Canyon plays a major spiritual role in Kawaiisu culture, as "the continued use of lands within the park for traditional cultural practices by the local Native American community sustains and reinforces the age-old knowledge manifested in the rock art and other cultural landscapes here" (p. 73). A recent paper on landscape archaeology in the western Mojave similarly points to the cosmological importance of the canyon (Allen 2010:19–20). The park preserves far more than archaeological sites.

Two appendices provide selected artifact illustrations, site photographs, and lists and location maps for the prehistoric and historic period sites within the park. The tables have limited research potential as they merely include site numbers, the dates when sites were recorded, the names of site recorders, and site types. While some data can be gleaned from careful reading of the site summaries, qualified researchers interested in details on site settings, site sizes, relevant artifact assemblages, or chronology will likely need to access data through the Department of Parks and Recreation and/or the Kern County Archaeological Information Center. The main purpose of the monograph is to provide a broad overview of the archaeological resources in the park rather than a detailed analysis of sites or artifact assemblages. The author is to be congratulated for bringing the significance of the cultural resources of Red Rock Canyon State Park and the extent of archaeological investigations there to the attention of both the public and Mojave Desert archaeologists.

References

Allen, Mark W.
   2011   Of Earth and Stone: Landscape Archaeology in the Mojave Desert. *California Archaeology* 3(1):11–30.
Faull, Mark R.
   2004   Cinema Red Rock: Contributions to the Myth of the American West by the Iconic Imagery of Red Rock Canyon, California. In Mark W. Allen and Judyth Reed (eds.) *The Human Journey and Ancient Life in the California's Deserts, Proceedings from the 2001 Millennium Conference*, pp. 299–306. Maturango Museum Publication No. 15. Ridgecrest, CA.

REVIEWS

Exploring Methods of Faunal Analysis: Insights from California Archaeology

Michael A. Glassow and Terry L. Joslin, editors

2012. Perspectives in California Archaeology Vol. 9. Cotsen Institute of Archaeology, University of California, Los Angeles. 258 pp, $34.95 (paper). ISBN-978-1-931745-87-1.

Review by R. Lee Lyman, University of Missouri-Columbia.

This volume consists of 13 chapters, each a case study, written by 18 authors (including the editors), plus introductory and concluding chapters by the editors. Many of the chapters were first presented at the 2006 ICAZ meeting, with five additional chapters being solicited. As the volume title indicates, the subject is methods of faunal analysis, and the geographic focus is California. Overall, the volume is an interesting read, with things that anyone undertaking zooarchaeological research will find informative and useful in a different geographic context. That is, the methods described are not particularly peculiar to California zoo-archaeology, despite claims of the editors and several authors to the contrary. Thus there is something here for almost anyone with a research interest in faunal remains recovered from archaeological sites. Many of the discussions concern shellfish or finny fish; a few concern mammals. Many chapters repeat the well-known fact that recovery techniques influence what we end up with for analysis. And a number of discussions concern quantification units and methods. Thus the *Exploring Methods* title is spot on, but of course the case-study aspect means there is also a wealth of substantive data here.

A critical method of zooarchaeology that is hardly mentioned concerns the taxonomic identification of faunal remains. With one terse exception (Gifford-Gonzalez and Hildebrandt's chapter on pinniped remains), discussion of why particular faunal remains are assigned to particular taxa is minimal. Virtually all chapters identify which comparative collections were consulted during identification, but a list of comparative collections doesn't indicate why the analyst thought bone X represents species Y. Which morphometric anatomical criteria were used to make identifications of particular bones, shells, and teeth? How do we know that some taxa represent a particular species of mouse, or cottontail, or deer, rather than some other species of mouse, or cottontail, or deer? The latter is particularly critical when we are told some bones represent *Lepus californicus* (Grimstead's chapter) and other specimens represent *Felis rufus* (Whitaker's chapter) when no biologist, paleontologist, or zooarchaeologist I know can distinguish skeletal remains of these taxa (unless they are of particular portions of the skull).

Taxonomic identification is the drudgery of the zooarchaeological enterprise,

California Archaeology, Volume 4, Number 2, December 2012, pp. 266–268.

but it is also the foundation of dietary and paleoecological inferences. The basis of Gobalet's identification of prehistoric coho salmon remains is obscure and thus the validity of his argument about prehistoric biogeography and modern conservation is compromised. Gobalet presents black and white photos of salmonid vertebrae without scales (not fish dermis, but information that allows us to discern how large illustrated vertebrae are) and without an indication of taxonomically diagnostic features. My colleague Virginia Butler (personal communication) believes that distinguishing salmonid species based on vertebrae is not possible, and based on research she and her colleagues have published (e.g., *Ancient Biomolecules* 2:17–26; *Journal of Archaeological Science* 38:136–146), I side with her rather than Gobalet.

The editors' claim that all archaeologists should be capable of basic faunal identification, by which I think they mean archaeologists should have the ability to sort birds from finny fish from mammal from shellfish remains. Although I don't doubt that sorting vertebrate from invertebrate remains is easily learned, sorting vertebrate remains into general taxonomic categories such as finny fish, birds, reptiles, and mammals has, in my experience, an accuracy rate of about 70%. It is not unusual to find bird and fish bone mixed in with what is alleged to be only mammal bone. The same goes for worked bone, bone that has intentionally been modified for purposes of making a tool; is this category of faunal remains (not mentioned in the volume under review) to be sorted out and not sent to a zooarchaeologist? And in these days of NAGPRA, I have to wonder about sorting out human remains; should this be done prior to a zooarchaeologist being sent a collection?

Statistical analyses range from non-existent in some chapters where a simple student's *t*-test would help immensely (Rick and Erlandson's chapter) to what seems like statistical overkill (Pletka's chapter), particularly given that the chapter immediately following the latter addresses the same analytical issue with minimal statistical analyses (Bertrando and McKenzie's chapter). Maps vary in quality, resolution and format from chapter to chapter. This is not damning, but it does sometimes make me wish for more detail and finer resolution in some maps. There are a minimum of typographical errors, but the tables accompanying one chapter are full of misspelled taxonomic names. That is disconcerting in a volume focused on zooarchaeology.

I was asked to review this volume because the editor thought "the perspective of a zooarchaeologist from outside of California would be especially valuable." I have worked on collections from both coastal and interior contexts in Oregon and Washington, so am not from far outside of California. Yet, as I read each chapter, particularly the summary chapter by the editors, I could not escape the feeling that if one does zooarchaeological research in California, then one does not read much of the zooarchaeological literature concerning other areas of North America or the world. Thus time after time statements like "bone fragmentation in California sites is not well understood" and "weight is a more valid measure of taxonomic abundance than NISP when California samples are small" are encountered. Although these statements also apply in Wisconsin, Brazil, France, and China, you certainly don't get that impression from this book. The subtitle of the book—*Insights from California Archaeology*—is not misleading with respect to the empirical data described and analyzed, but in terms of methods the volume is parochial in the sense of the limited techniques discussed. That is unfortunate from the perspective of someone working outside the area.

In sum, *Exploring Methods of Faunal Analysis* contains exemplary analyses of taxonomically diverse collections and illustrates a plethora of analytical methods. Assuming it represents the state of zooarchaeological science in California, there is much to be proud of. But there is also room for improvement. I look forward to tracking the latter in the future.

REVIEWS

Polynesians in America: Pre-Columbian Contacts with the New World

Terry L. Jones, Alice A. Storey, Elizabeth Matisoo-Smith, and Jose Miguel Ramirez-Aliaga, editors

2011. AltaMira Press, Lanham, Maryland, xix + 359 pp. $85.00 (cloth). ISBN 978-0-7591-2004-4

Reviewed by Patrick V. Kirch, University of California, Berkeley

Transoceanic bridge or daunting barrier? These opposing views of the Pacific Ocean have inspired scholarly debates regarding the possibility of pre-Columbian connections between Polynesia and the New World for more than a century. Claims for such contacts were first put forward in the early nineteenth century, but without doubt the most famous arguments were put forward by the Norwegian explorer Thor Heyerdahl in the mid-twentieth century. To "prove" his theory that South American Indians had populated Eastern Polynesia, in 1947 Heyerdahl drifted on the balsa raft *Kon-Tiki* from Peru to the Tuamotu Islands. Decades of subsequent research have failed to produce any body of archaeological, linguistic, or human biological data that would support the contention that the Polynesians derived from South America.

On the other hand there is strong evidence that at least one important crop plant of South American origins, the sweet potato (*Ipomoea batatas*), had been introduced to Eastern Polynesia in pre-European contact times. Ethnobotanist Douglas Yen advanced this argument in 1974, and in 1989 Patrick Kirch and John Hather published on carbonized sweet potato tuber remains from Mangaia Island, radiocarbon dated to ca. AD 1000–1100. Arguments have also been made that the bottle gourd (*Lagenaria siceraria*), widely used in Eastern Polynesia, was similarly introduced from the Americas. That there was some form of pre-Columbian *contact* between Polynesia and South America seems undisputed; the precise nature of that contact, however, is an open question.

Polynesians in America, stemming from a symposium held at the annual meeting of the Society for American Archaeology in St. Louis in 2010, addresses from fresh perspectives the question of contacts between Polynesia and the New World. The authors bring a range of mostly new archaeological, linguistic, ethnographic, and biological evidence to bear on this topic.

The first four chapters, some 70 pages in all, consist of introductory essays. Jones introduces the case for Polynesian contacts in Chapter 1. Along with a brief review of earlier literature, he points out that the current authors are not claiming "intercivilizational cultural exchanges" across the Pacific (such as between China and Mesoamerica), but only "contact between Polynesian seafarers of the Pacific and Native societies of the west coast of the Americas" (p. 6). Chapter 2, by Storey and Jones, follows with a detailed consideration of *diffusion* in American archaeological theory. As they recount, diffusionism has had its ups and downs over the years as different paradigms have come and gone in archaeology. They are at pains to point out that one must distinguish "wild-eyed hyperdiffusionist arguments" from closely reasoned cases of "occasional cultural contacts" based on multiple lines of evidence (p. 23). In Chapter 3, Jones and Storey review mythological accounts of contacts from both Polynesia and Americas, but find that most of the "mythological parallels are vague and often impossible to evaluate critically" (p. 35). In the rather lengthy Chapter 4, Jones and Storey recount in greater detail the history of anthropological debate regarding Polynesia-America connections.

Beginning with Chapter 5, by Jones, the book starts to focus in on actual evidence and case studies of contact. Jones reviews the artifact record from North America, concentrating on fishhooks and sewn-plank boat technology. He argues that both of these technologies are likely to have been adopted by North American coastal groups due to contacts with seafaring Polynesians, at two different time periods (ca. AD 700 and 1300 respectively). Ramirez-Aliaga (Chapter 6) looks at evidence for connections between the Mapuche people of southern Chile and Polynesians, such as clubs and stone adzes; the likelihood that the Mapuche term for adze, *toki*, is borrowed from Polynesian is quite striking.

In Chapter 7, Storey, Clarke, and Matisoo-Smith examine evidence for various commensal species being transferred between Polynesia and the Americas, primarily sweet potato and bottle gourd from South America to Polynesia, and the domestic chicken in the opposite direction. This is followed in Chapter 8 by a reappraisal of the recent claims for a pre-Columbian introduction of chickens into the Americas (Storey, Quiroz, and Matisoo-Smith). The initial publication in 2007 of purported pre-Columbian chicken bones from the El Arenal site in Chile provoked a heated debate, hence the extended presentation and discussion of archaeological, radiocarbon, and aDNA evidence here is most welcome. Although the controversy is likely to continue, the authors reassert their position that the chicken bones from El Arenal are "clearly pre-Columbian" (p. 168). This would seem to join the well-dated samples of sweet potato remains from Mangaia as some of the strongest evidence for Polynesian-American contacts.

Two chapters invoke linguistic evidence for contact. Scaglion and Cordero in Chapter 9 build a case on ethnographic and linguistic grounds that the Gulf of Guayaquil in Ecuador was a locus of contact, although they readily admit that their scenario is "speculative" (p. 192). In Chapter 10, Klar argues that certain North American words, especially that for sewn-plank boat (*tomol*) are Polynesian borrowings. But Klar acknowledges that "there remains much to be done in the search for linguistic evidence of Polynesian-American contact" (p. 207).

Matisoo-Smith (Chapter 11) turns to human biological evidence that some of the purported Polynesian voyagers may have remained, or left their genes, in the Americas. She describes particularly intriguing skeletal evidence from Mocha Island which one hopes will soon be followed up with aDNA analysis.

Much of the debate over purported contacts rides on issues of chronology. The timing of Polynesian colonization of the southeastern islands and archipelagoes has been a matter of some controversy, reviewed in Chapter 12 by Weisler and Green. They conclude that this vast region was explored and settled between ca. AD 800–1000, which sets an important time frame since contact with South America is therefore unlikely to have predated this period. Irwin follows this in Chapter 13 with a discussion of canoe capabilities and possible sailing routes.

All of the authors join in a Summary and Conclusions (Chapter 14). Perhaps their most important point is the power of multi-disciplinary collaborations (between archaeology, genetics, linguistics, physical anthropology, and so on) to understand the nature of pre-Columbian culture contacts "without resorting to the racist and outlandish conclusions of the early 1900s" (p. 276). Although the debate will no doubt continue for years to come, this book is a most welcome contribution to that approach.

NEWS AND NOTES

Compiled by Shelly Davis-King, Davis-King & Associates,
P.O. Box 10, Standard, CA 95373

News and Notes looks to the readership for direction, ideas, and contributions about archaeological issues, unusual artifacts, fieldwork summaries, important new legislation, and memories about our colleagues who have passed on. In this issue, a possible bighorn sheep hunting area is reported in the high Sierra Nevada, an anthropomorphic stone figurine from Owens Lake is described, and *Sands of Time* recognizes Clem Meighan.

The Monument Ridge Bighorn Sheep Hunting Locale

During my (Jack Scott's) tenure on the Bridgeport Ranger District, Humboldt-Toiyabe National Forest, archaeological research has focused on both historic (i.e., mining, logging activities, and Chinese occupation) and prehistoric (i.e., big game hunting and obsidian use) resources. In the summer of 2007, while looking for historic era mining sites above the Green Creek drainage in Mono County, Clifford Shaw (Bridgeport Ranger District, Humboldt-Toiyabe National Forest volunteer) discovered a possible big game procurement site that consisted of six hunting blinds and a possible lookout in association with a rock alignment and two segments of a wood alignment that may constitute a drift fence (Figure 1). Several obsidian flakes and one broken obsidian projectile point were also located at that time..

Figure 1. Clifford Shaw examining one of the Monument Ridge hunting blinds. (Photograph by Jack Scott).

California Archaeology, Volume 4, Number 2, December 2012, pp. 273–293.

273

Overview

Upon review of the site's features and artifacts, as well as discussions with the Bridgeport Ranger District Wildlife biologist, we hypothesized that it was a bighorn sheep hunting locale. To our knowledge, this is the first of this site type to be located by archaeologists in the Sierra Nevada. California Department of Fish and Game personnel have noted hunting blinds in the Baxter Pass area, just west of Independence, California (Tom Stephenson, personal communication 2008). Another possible bighorn sheep procurement area was recorded by Crystal West (2010) near Mount Williamson.

Site Description

The site is located above an open, low, sage-covered chute on Monument Ridge, overlooking the Green Creek drainage (Figure 2). It is approximately 390 m north-south by 300 m east-west and varies in elevation from 2,965 to 3,005 m above mean sea level. The "drift fence" is approximately 350 m long and consists of "improvements" made to naturally occurring rock outcrops. These improvements include a short rock alignment section that is approximately 15 m long, and two wood alignment sections, one 40 m long and the other 35 m in length. The wood from the latter alignments is burned around the base, varies in length up to 2.5 m, and is less than 10 cm in diameter. These alignments are located where there are

Figure 2. Rock alignment with Green Creek in background. (Photograph by Jack Scott.)

breaks in natural rock outcrops between the hunting blinds. Additional inventory of the site led to the discovery of less than 30 tertiary obsidian flakes and four broken obsidian projectile points/bifaces, situated between four and 20 m from the hunting blinds. Only one of the flakes was within a hunting blind.

John Muir observed and later described Indians hunting bighorn sheep on Mount Grant near Walker Lake, Nevada, "where considerable numbers of Indians used to hunt together, being perfectly acquainted with the topography and habits and instincts of game were very successful." He further described "nest-like enclosures built of stones" (Muir 1894:238) on the summits of mountains in Nevada. When startled, the sheep instinctively headed to the uplands where they could observe their surroundings, thus coming into range of the Indian hunters. Muir (1894:238) also observed and described a bighorn sheep trap consisting of a high-walled corral with guiding wing fences, into which the game was driven by great numbers of Indians and then slaughtered (similar to pronghorn traps described by Steward [1938:34] used during communal hunts). According to the Washoe Tribal Historic Preservation Officer, Darrel Cruz (personal communication 2008), the Washoe—who hunted bighorn sheep further north in the Sierra—were "a chosen few and mighty hunters."

Discussion

Bighorn sheep have adapted to utilizing steep rocky cliffs, benches, and bowls that are visually open for foraging, as well as chutes that are used as venues between foraging areas and escape routes to upper elevation lookouts. This Monument Ridge hunting area is located at the end of a chute above rocky cliffs, and utilizes natural terrain. We believe that the prehistoric drift fence and hunting blinds found at this location, along with the natural terrain features of the area, made this site an ideal location for bighorn sheep procurement. If hunters approached the bighorn sheep foraging below Monument Ridge, the sheep would instinctively proceed up the open chute toward higher ground and along the drift fence, whereupon they would pass in front of the blinds where the concealed hunters could dispatch the animals. Based on the paucity of projectile points, it appears that this hunting locale was used infrequently, possibly by single or small groups of hunters.

References Cited

Muir, John
    1894   *The Mountains of California*. The Century Company, New York.

NEWS AND NOTES

Steward, Julian

   1938   *Basin-Plateau Aboriginal Sociopolitical Groups.* Bureau of American Ethnology Bulletin 120, Washington, D.C.

West, Crystal

   2010   The "Ridge Place": Prehistoric Use of Ridgelines along the Sierra Escarpment above the Owens Valley. Paper presented at the 44th Annual Meeting of the Society for California Archaeology, Riverside.

David J. "Jack" Scott with Clifford Shaw and Leeann Murphy
BLM Alturas Field Office, Alturas, California
and Leeann Murphy
Inyo National Forest, Bishop, CA

Owens Lake Carved Stone Figurine-Fertility Effigy

In 2011, a carved prehistoric anthropomorphic stone figurine (P14-011588) was discovered on the surface of a historic sand beach strandline on the south side of Point Bartlett of Owens Lake, at elevation of 1,090.5 m (3,577.8 ft). This isolate was observed during investigations by a team of archaeologists represented by Garcia and Associates and BonTerra, and geologists from MWH Global in support of the Los Angeles Department of Water and Power's Owens Lake Dust Mitigation and Monitoring Project (Denardo et al. 2012). No additional artifacts were identified in the area surrounding the figurine and the nearest archaeological site is approximately 152 m (500 ft) away.

The small, lightweight, hand-carved artifact measures approximately 4.0 × 3.0 × 2.5 cm (Figure 1). When found, a layer of mud covered the surface of the figurine. Microscopy and raw material comparative (provenance) analysis indicates that the specimen was carved from lightly welded volcanic tuff from the Alabama Hills Volcanic Complex (Javl) which outcrops near the northwest corner of Owens Lake; thus, it is likely that it was carved locally. Given that this isolated artifact is not associated with any archaeological sites or temporally diagnostic artifacts, it was not possible to date it. As a result, the figurine could be several thousand years old, or it could date as late as the twentieth century.

The figurine appears to be a female in a squatting position giving birth. There is a blanket pattern on her back and she appears to be holding a cup, bowl, or mortar in her hands, which are enlarged and may represent wings or fins. The anthropomorphic figure appears to have a bird-like head with a flat, duck-like bill and a tall collar (Figure 2). What appears to be the head of a newborn child has either a pronounced lower chin or a duck bill.

Results of cursory research to locate similar carved stone figurines in the

Figure 1. Front view (left) and side view (right) of carved stone figurine. Photograph by Maryann Thomas.

Figure 2. Back view (left) and close-up (right) of carved stone figurine. Photograph by Carole Denardo.

Owens Lake area, the homeland of Paiute-Shoshone groups, were negative. Steatite zoomorphic effigies and human phallic representations are known from the Channel Islands area of the southern California coast, although stone anthropomorphic figures are noticeably absent (Hudson and Blackburn 1980). An examination of Great Basin prehistoric cultures also provides examples of stone zoomorphic effigies, particularly in western Nevada, represented by slate, scoria, and vesicular basalt figures (Tuohy 1986). Strong (1969) depicted miniature stone and bone effigies from the western Great Basin, including both zoomorphic and anthropomorphic figurines (Strong 1969: Figures 105 and 106).

More common are fired and unfired clay effigies in eastern California and throughout the Great Basin region. Numerous unfired anthropomorphic figures have been identified in Death Valley and there is evidence that Southern Paiute children fashioned clay human and animal figurines for play (Kelly and Fowler 1986:381). A pregnant woman clay effigy has also been reported in Plumas County, California (Tuohy 1986), but nothing similar to the Owens Lake stone figurine has been identified.

The function of the Owens Lake carved stone figurine is speculative, but it was not likely for use as a toy by children. A tentative interpretation may coincide with a creation story for a prehistoric culture focused on wetland/lake bird food procurement, or it may be associated with fertility rituals due to a concern for fecundity. Although no Paiute or Shoshone mythological tales were identified that could provide clues regarding the function of this artifact, a Washoe creation tale features "Old Woman," a female mallard duck who, along with her brothers (Weasel, Wolf, and Coyote), was responsible for creating the world and human beings (Hudson 1902:238-239; also see d'Azevedo 1986:489). However, despite the possible linkage with this creation tale, as with other forms of rock art, we can only surmise when and why this figurine was created.

References Cited

d'Azevedo, Warren L.
  1986   The Washoe. In *Handbook of North American Indians*, Volume 11, Great Basin, edited by
          Warren L. d'Azevedo, pp. 466–498. Smithsonian Institution, Washington, D.C.
Denardo, Carole, Rachael Greenlee, Matthew J. Steinkamp
  2012   Final Report: Owens Lake Dust Mitigation Program, Phase 7a, Phase II Archaeological
          Testing and Evaluation, Owens Lake, Inyo County, California. Report on file with the Los
          Angeles Department of Water and Power, Los Angeles, California.
Hudson, J. W. H.
  1902   Unpublished Field Notes on the Washoe, Northern Paiute, Owens Valley Paiute, etc.
          Unpublished manuscript and collections catalog in the Field Museum of Natural History,
          Chicago.

Hudson, Travis, and Thomas C. Blackburn

    1980   *The Material Culture of the Chumash Interaction Sphere, Volume IV: Ceremonial Parapher-nalia, Games, and Amusements.* Ballena Press, Menlo Park, California, and Santa Barbara Museum of Natural History, Santa Barbara, California.

Kelly, Isabel T., and Catherine S. Fowler

    1986   Southern Paiute. In *Handbook of North American Indians*, Volume 11, Great Basin, edited by Warren L. d'Azevedo, pp. 368–397. Smithsonian Institution, Washington, D.C.

Strong, Emory

    1969   *Stone Age in the Great Basin.* Binfords & Mort Publishers, Portland, Oregon.

Tuohy, Donald R.

    1986   Portable Art Objects. In *Handbook of North American Indians*, Volume 11, Great Basin, edited by Warren L. d'Azevedo, pp. 227–237. Smithsonian Institution, Washington, D.C.

Carole Denardo, Garcia and Associates

Government News

Bureau of Indian Affairs

The Tejon Indian Tribe became federally "re-recognized" by the U.S. Department of the Interior, Bureau of Indian Affairs (BIA) in January 2012. In a letter dated January 3, 2012, from Assistant Secretary–Indian Affairs Larry Echo Hawk, the BIA wrote that "an administrative error" had omitted the tribe from the Federal Register under "Indian Entities Recognized and Eligible to Receive Services from the United States Bureau of Indian Affairs" and that they were now reinstated. The Assistant Secretary–Indian Affairs discharges the duties of the Secretary of the Interior with the authority and direct responsibility to strengthen the government-to-government relationship with the nation's 566 federally recognized tribes, advocates policies that support Indian self-determination, protects and preserves Indian trust assets, and administers a wide array of laws, regulations, and functions relating to American Indian and Alaska Native tribes, tribal members, and individual trust beneficiaries. The Assistant Secretary oversees the BIA and the Bureau of Indian Education. Recognition of the Tejon Indian Tribe brings the total number of California tribes recognized by the federal government to 108. A new list of federally recognized tribes was published in the Federal Register on August 10, 2012, and can be found at 75 CFR 60810.

Bureau of Land Management

In June 2012, the Bureau of Land Management (BLM) implemented a new Programmatic Agreement (PA) among the BLM, the Advisory Council on Historic Preservation, and the National Conference of State Historic Preservation Officers

"Regarding the Manner in Which the BLM Will Meet its Responsibilities Under the National Historic Preservation Act." The PA can be found at www.blm.gov/wo/st/en/prog/more/CRM/blm_preservation_board/prog_agreement.html.

Sands of Time: SCA's Past

Memories of Clement Woodward Meighan (1925–1997)
Compiled and edited by Michael J. Moratto and Keith L. Johnson

Clem Meighan's life was legendary: He was a child prodigy; war hero; brilliant university student; inspirational professor; world-class scientist; outstanding scholar, author, and mentor; devoted family man; humorist; and truly one of the founding fathers of California archaeology. As summed up in Brian Dillon's homage, "Clem Meighan was the best there ever was. He made it all look so easy" (Dillon 2005:9). Notable aspects of Clem's career are highlighted in the two memorial volumes prepared by many of his friends, former colleagues, and students (Dillon and Boxt 2005; Johnson 2005). Briefly, he was born in San Francisco, raised in impoverished circumstances there as well as in Phoenix and Turlock, and then drafted into the U.S. Army at the height of World War II. Gravely wounded by machine gun fire on Saipan in 1944, Meighan spent nearly three years recuperating in military hospitals. He then blazed his way through the undergraduate and graduate programs at UC Berkeley, and by 1952 was hired as an instructor in the anthropology department at UCLA.

Figure 1. Old friends Clem Meighan (left) and Frank Fenenga on the Kings River, Fresno County, summer 1983. Photograph by Brian Dervin Dillon.

With his characteristic drive and focus, Clem quickly rose through the faculty ranks, became department head, and pursued field research not only in California but also in other western states, Baja California, central and western Mexico, Belize, Costa Rica, Guam, Okinawa, Nubia, and Syria. Along the way, he established the UCLA Archaeological Survey and Rock Art Archive, and published more than 300 scholarly books, articles, and monographs. He was a pioneer in studies of southern California archaeology, rock art, obsidian hydration dating, "early man" in America, cultural ecology, and the prehistory of the southern Channel Islands. Perhaps his greatest legacy, however, was in providing a superb education for countless undergraduate and graduate students, many of whom went on to pursue distinguished careers of their own in archaeology and allied disciplines. In their reminiscences below, the essence of Clement Meighan lives on.

Michael J. Moratto
Applied EarthWorks, Inc.
Westlake Village, California

References Cited

Dillon, Brian D.
  2005   In Memoriam: Clement Woodward Meighan, 1925-1997. In *Onward and Upward: Papers in Honor of Clement W. Meighan*, edited by Keith L. Johnson, pp. 3-9. Stansbury Publishing, Chico, California.
Dillon, Brian D., and Matthew A. Boxt (editors)
  2005   *Archaeology without Limits: Papers in Honor of Clement W. Meighan*. Labyrinthos, Lancaster, California.
Johnson, Keith L. (editor)
  2005   *Onward and Upward: Papers in Honor of Clement W. Meighan*. Stansbury Publishing, Chico, California.

Clem Awakens the Mountain Spirits   Thirty years ago, in the late summer of 1983, Clem Meighan was revisiting locations from his first season of archaeological fieldwork. I had been an "all-but-dissertation" graduate student at UC Berkeley when Clem hired me to come south and work at UCLA, but now my four-year research position had just come to an end. As a means of keeping me on, and bringing in my own salary, Clem had helped me land a federal contract to revisit archaeological sites on the Kern, Tule, and Kings rivers he had recorded prior to dam construction exactly 36 years earlier.

Four years before that, as soon he turned 19, Clem had been drafted out of UC Berkeley and sent off to war. Many of his peers, including H. B. Nicholson and my own father, likewise left UC Berkeley to fight in World War II as teenagers.

As a U.S. Army tanker in support of the U.S. Marine assault on Saipan in 1944, Clem was badly wounded. Hit by three machine-gun bullets after his tank blew up, Meighan was rescued under fire but subsequently left with the dead and dying at the forward aid station. By chance he was the last wounded man taken off the beach that day and sent offshore to a hospital ship.

Clem spent the next three years in military hospitals, including Tripler in Honolulu and Letterman at the San Francisco Presidio. During his long recovery, Clem re-enrolled at UC Berkeley and began studying archaeology. Released from the hospital in 1947, but not yet completely healed, Meighan began fieldwork in the Sierra Nevada foothills that summer—his first full season of archaeology. More significantly, with his new career he finally left behind the land of the dead and dying.

One of my 1983 contract obligations was, at Clem's suggestion, "consultation." This allowed me to tag along while "elder statesmen" of California archaeology tripped down memory lane. The justification was that since these persons had been the first scientific visitors at some of the sites I was re-recording, nobody was better qualified to assess the degree of damage suffered, or alternatively, preservation sustained, by the archaeological sites initially documented long before I was born. It was a special treat for Clem to get together with his old friend, Frank Fenenga, in Fresno County again. Clem's first academic interest had been entomology, and at 16 he was the youngest member of the California Academy of Sciences. It had been Fenenga more than any other person who convinced Clem to leave his bugs behind and switch to archaeology. Clem's initial fieldwork season in California archaeology during the summer of 1947 was at Frank Fenenga's invitation.

Almost a half-century before the 1983 episode, in the mid-1930s, Franklin Fenenga had been one of the younger, if not the youngest, person ever hired to do Depression-era archaeology for the Smithsonian Institution/Works Progress Administration. At age 16, Frank was running crews of more than 100 diggers, most of them female, all of them barefoot, in the Deep South. After the war, Fenenga was the archaeologist to see when the River Basin Surveys were finally extended to California. Meighan and Fenenga were lifelong friends and enjoyed an erudite joking relationship. Clem always referred to (Frisian) Fenenga as "the only Irishman too dumb to spell '*Finnegan*,' his real last name," while Fenenga usually responded that Clem's patronymic was actually "*Meegian*," because he was an "Armenian fig-grower from Fresno" masquerading as an Irish Turlockian.

I was also able to rope in another of Clem's closest friends from his Berkeley years, Fritz Riddell. Since "Frank" was already taken, it was Fenenga who had bestowed Riddell's postwar UC *nom de guerre* of "Fritz." All three old buddies greatly enjoyed whooping it up around my 1983 campfire. *The California Drinking Song*, a staple of Berkeley undergraduates in the '30s and '40s was sung in four-part har-

mony in 1983, with Fritz Riddell denying vociferously—but not convincingly—
that the opening stanza (*"Oh we had to carry Harry to the Ferry..."*) referred to his
older brother and fellow archaeologist, Harry Riddell. After Meighan, Fenenga,
Riddell, and Dillon recited passages from Mel Brook's classic *Blazing Saddles* mov-
ie, and all but Clem agreed that *UCLA* stood for "University of California for Lower
Achievers," the campfire conversation shifted to Robert F. Heizer, our contemporary at UC Berkeley. All four of us were unencumbered by any personal affection
for Heizer. The consensus of opinion was that Heizer divided the human population into only two categories: potential victims on the one hand, and potential
competitors (and therefore, by default, enemies) on the other. Fenenga, Meighan,
and Riddell all had been entered onto Heizer's "marked for death" enemies list
since the mid-1950s; my own name was added two decades after theirs.

The next morning, Riddell returned to Sacramento to tilt at his bureaucratic
windmills, abandoning Clem and Frank to my care. After hitting Trimmer Springs
and inspecting various Kings River bedrock mortar sites, Clem told me that he
wanted to revisit Balch Camp, the site that had originally kindled his interest in
California rock art. Neither Meighan nor Fenenga had been back to the place since
1947, and both were pleased, proud, and not a little surprised to see how well
the unusual large-scale human outline pictographs had held up over the decades.
The dusty clearing of 1947 had been replaced by an asphalt parking lot, and the
rock face, naturally protected by the overhang of the granite boulder, was further
protected now by a split rail fence to keep urbanites from ramming it. The two old
friends approached the rock art panel, conversing in low tones, lost in their memories of a much earlier time in California archaeology, the here and now completely
forgotten. Clem and Frank stepped over the low fence and each put a hand on
the boulder, so as to lean closer and inspect the familiar pictographs and see how
much they had changed since their last visit.

The instant flesh met stone, the wind kicked up, thunder boomed in the distance, and a gentle rain began. The weather change came so suddenly, it was almost as if the spirits residing within the boulder marked by ancient rock art had
been set free by the two giants of California archaeology. The pictographs had
called Clem back, and the mountain spirits, slumbering for many years, possibly
since 1947, now had made their presence known. The two old friends had awak-
ened them, effortlessly, in the most natural way, by their pilgrimage to the location which had such great meaning to them both. And the spirits, commanding
the wind, rain, and thunder, celebrated Clem's return to the place where his life as
an archaeologist had begun.

Brian Dervin Dillon, Consulting Archaeologist,
North Hills, California

A Kindred Spirit   I remember Clem not only as a great mentor and a good friend but also as a kindred spirit as regards his perspective on life. I never heard him utter the words to which I so often give voice now, as I did then, but I am sure that his belief was the same as mine: if you don't keep laughing, you'll very soon be crying, and life will be, as he used to put it, just a guano sandwich. He leavened the work of excavation with humor day after day throughout the years when we worked together, usually with a feigned sort of hayseed-rube manner that was enough in itself to get us all laughing. I cannot remember a night in the field that did not begin with one-liners that he bellowed out in the darkness as the rest of us were on the point of falling asleep. The cry of "Baaeeeyah!!! And from the dark and stormy night came a horrendous cry..." was enough to start us guffawing, even when it was repeated night after night, for we knew the rest of the off-color sentence by heart.

Beyond that, Clem kept the tradition of music in the field alive with his ever-present concertina. He told me once that with no particular musical background, he chose the concertina because it was easily portable, fit into a very small space, and appeared easy to play. Of course, that appearance was a bit deceptive, but still he mastered enough of the little squeeze-box to give us something to sing with when work was done. I tried, after a time, to join him on the banjo, but we never managed to get the two instruments into something approximating tune, not even close enough to serve for folk music. As a result, he and I (and others) usually took solo turns playing while the group sang—a tradition that, sad to say, has very nearly died out in today's world of multiple iPods around digs, each individual ear-phoned in to his or her favorite brand of music. I find the blank, uncomprehending stares of students rather hard to take when I begin to extol the virtues of live music in the evenings as opposed to today's canned stuff, and I am sure that Clem would have been just as disturbed by the passing of the mutual, though not always entirely tuneful, efforts of those years long ago.

Comedy is partly a matter of material, but mostly a matter of timing. Clem had material in copious quantity, and like any great comedian he was capable of grasping a moment and making it his own with a skillfully timed shot of humor. Once, en route to a field camp where I was with a group of other students, he passed through Stockton around 2:00 A.M. and witnessed a scene that he recreated for us when he arrived, and many a time thereafter, never failing to adorn the tale with bursts of laughter. He had spied a man rounding a corner and running toward him at full speed, and the reason for his flight became apparent when a woman appeared behind him, brandishing a large knife. As she ran, she burst out with "I'm gonna cut your heart out, you sentimental sonofabitch!!!," a line that became one of Clem's great stock of such things in the years that followed.

But of all the times when his sterling qualities came to the fore, none sticks as solidly in my memory as a moment in the summer of 1953 when he and I were searching for the owner of a piece of acreage that Clem wanted to survey. We finally found the owner at a gate to his fields, where he had stopped his stake-side cattle truck. We stood beside the truck as Clem explained what we wanted to do, while behind the vehicle's openwork sides the cattle began to get restless. Before long, one of them deposited a load of solid waste on the truck's floor, and part of it spattered out and onto Clem. The owner said, "Oh jeez, you got some on you! I'm real sorry," to which Clem, without a second's hesitation, replied "Don't worry about it; I've been shat on by experts." I will be forever grateful to him for showing me not only how to do archaeological fieldwork but also that such labor can truly be fun—if one is with the right people.

David M. Pendergast
Honorary Senior Research Fellow, Institute of Archaeology
University College London

Always Look on the Bright Side of Life   Before meeting Clem Meighan, the most influential professor I ever had in the field of archaeology, I'd like to go back a few years before attending UCLA. I was always a history buff and during a class in high school, I took on a challenge from my teacher, who said that the California coastal Indians were lazy and unproductive. I disagreed with him and then had to produce a research paper to prove that his assumptions were wrong. He was fair at admitting that he was misinformed and had learned something new. After this experience, I'd been bitten by the "archaeology bug." This led to numerous visits, especially to Anasazi sites and museums around the Southwest. By this time, archaeology had become fully possessive of my future plans.

After completing junior college, I transferred to UCLA in the fall semester 1953. My first contact with Clem began with his spring semester (1954) Anthropology 106 class on the Archaeology of North American Indians. This was supplemented with his Anthropology 195 class on Methods in Field Archaeology. His enthusiasm was so catching that I decided then and there to become a "dirt archaeologist." Right from the start, Clem gave us the feeling of being on the team. He was a learning-by-doing teacher. Not only did he teach us proper excavation techniques, such as how to use a shovel and other digging tools, how to keep profiles straight and plumb, the use of different surveying methods and field photography, but also the keen analytical observations of site situations and the importance of artifact interpretation and stratigraphy. For him, it was like an open book. If you read it properly, it would give you an insight into the historical picture unfolding before you. I think his motto for us was something like the U.S. Marine's "Semper Fi" (always faithful)—"Sigi Sigi Trabajo" (work, work, work!).

Clem's sense of humor and comradeship were famous. He was one of us, although he was the professor. His anecdotes and stories were always the spice in the soup. For example, there was the story of his experiences while excavating the contents of a 19th century San Francisco "outhouse." Disregarding the odors (we didn't ask if he had used a gas mask), he was able to date the arrival of Chinese laborers by the increased number of porcelain sherds found in the deposits.

Another humorous incident took place during the 1954 field school in Paragonah, Utah (his first major field school at UCLA). The local press came one day to report on our excavation progress. That year, a very distinguished-looking elder member of the crew, Henry "Hutch" Hutchinson from Delaware, was "identified" as the professor and he played his role perfectly, while Clem stood most amused in the background. Clem's musical talents were also present. He often got out his concertina and we all sang along.

Clem also saw the potential in his students and encouraged them to publish jointly with him. This was the case, for example, with the publication in 1956 of the first Paragonah excavation (1954) report (*University of Utah Anthropological Papers* 25) in which he let me write a chapter.

We all admired Clem for his tolerance. You never saw a sign of hard feelings against anyone. When Hiroe Takamiya from Okinawa came to study archaeology under Meighan, although they had been "enemies" in World War II, there was no animosity—just common ground interests in the subject. You just couldn't help liking Hiroe.

Under Clem's direction, other excavations and surveys followed: the second field school at Paragonah in 1955, San Diego County, etc. Some were real (and dangerous) adventures. There was the Inyo County rockshelter dig, where all of the crew came down with valley fever (coccidioidomycosis). It almost killed Mark Kowta, and the rest of us were guinea pigs for the UCLA medical center for quite a while. Worse than that, we found a tobacco tin at the site, with a note saying that the artifacts, which we didn't find, were located in the UCLA collections; bad luck for a week's work. Then there was Santa Catalina Island, where after a bumpy flight over, we had to come back on a launch because of fog. We almost got gassed from the engine fumes. Also, while on site survey near Santa Barbara, we came out of the brush covered with ticks. Nevertheless, we all survived these perils.

In the fall of 1957, I was drafted into the U.S. Army and was sent to Germany in 1958. There I got in contact with the Friedrich Alexander University, in Erlangen (near Nürnberg). In 1959, I took part in excavating a paleolithic site near the Danube River in Bavaria, while still in the Army. After being discharged in 1960,

I went on to study European archaeology at this university. As a result of Clem's thorough training, I was able to teach a whole generation of archaeologists his systematic methods. Most of the professors I encountered let either students or laborers do the work for them without any proper training. Some of them even forbid their students to take part on digs until they had graduated. (Thank goodness, this has since greatly changed.) Although my commitment to field work ended in the mid-1970s, the training I received under Dr. Meighan prepared me in many ways for a future as a museum consultant.

Clem and I always tried to stay in contact, and when I was in California I tried to see him and Joan or at least talk to them on the telephone. As I followed his career, I felt that he was always open to new ideas and methods. He once told me that someone had donated a computer to the department and he was practically one of the first to see its potential and use it. Later he told me that he even took one to his Channel Island digs where it typed his daily reports. He said he didn't know how he typed all his early manuscripts (although he could type faster than most secretaries). He said he would come home, edit his notes, and then press the button and print it.

In summing up my thoughts on Clement Meighan, an old saying from one of my math teachers comes to mind: "Good, better, best; never let it rest, until the good is better and the better best." Another thought that would have fit him as well is a song performed by the British Monty Python Comedy Group (1969 to 1983): "Always look on the bright side of life." That was Clem—scholar, teacher, humorist and most of all, friend!

Dr. rer. nat. Frank D. Davis
Retired Archaeologist and Natural History
Museum Consultant for the State of Bavaria, Munich, Germany

The Past Belongs to All of Us   Clement W. Meighan was a graduate of the University of California, Berkeley, an anthropologist at the University of California, Los Angeles, initiator of the UCLA Archaeological Survey in 1957, and founder of the UCLA Rock Art Archive in 1977. Clem's UCLA colleague James (Jim) Sackett believes that the Survey was the "material core" around which the then-named Institute of Archaeology was formed in 1973. "The intellectual core was provided by the synergy Giorgio Bucellatti (the Institute's founder and first director) and Clem forged" to create a "cross-disciplinary scholarly ecumenicalism" characterizing today's Cotsen Institute of Archaeology. This quote from Jim, and others here, are from a file we have in the Archive entitled, "Clement W. Meighan, 1925-1997."

I first encountered Clem in 1976, six years before I entered the archaeology program. Anchored by a modest donation, the Archive was based then in Kinsey Hall. Even though Clem was involved with other Institute labs, the Archive had his full attention. He engaged UCLA supporter Franklin D. Murphy and encouraged volunteers, of which I was one. He reached out to colleagues, state officials, and researchers for donations of data collections. He created policy guidelines still viable in the digital world. Clem penned a brief history of the Archive in his "Theory and Practice in the History of Rock Art," included in a 1981 UCLA volume dedicated to Franklin D. Murphy.

With Clem's encouragement, I created an exhibition of images from Archive collections in collaboration with the U. S. National Park Service. Entitled "Shamans' Songs: the Rock Art of Western America," the exhibition toured parks throughout the west. This outreach was emulated in 2005 when the Archive contributed images to the Fowler Museum of Cultural History exhibition "UCLA Collects! Bodies of Knowledge."

In 1981, Clem and I collaborated to secure a modest grant from the California Council of the Humanities. The grant funded lectures and workshops exploring one central query: what is the relevance of rock art to the disciplines of anthropology and archaeology? Clem's opinion was that rock art studies should be interdisciplinary, but that rock art site data must be anchored within archaeological contexts. He secured for the Archive copies of California site records and reports on which rock art had been annotated but rarely investigated.

We followed up with a major grant from the Ahmanson Foundation. This allowed us to publish, in 1983, a catalog of our exhibit entitled *Ancient Images on Stone*. Clem's preface stated that "it is our hope that greater public awareness" of rock art would encourage its recognition as "an important part of our national heritage." This view, that the past belonged to all citizens, was one of Clem's bedrock professional values.

Another of Clem's finer qualities was his fondness for generous personal gestures. He followed up the success of our foray into public outreach by giving me his personal copy of *Cave Paintings of Baja California*, a collector's edition published by Dawson Books reporting his excavations in the painted caves of the Sierra de San Francisco. Taking this lovely book from the shelf in his office, with no hope of securing a replacement, he signed it and gave it to me with a grin.

Clem collaborated closely with C.W. Clewlow, Jr., on Archive matters and encouraged archaeology program students to pursue ancient aesthetics. Ellen Hardy followed her interest to Costa Rica, Georgia Lee to Easter Island, and David S. Whitley to California's Coso Range. My interest in rock art was redirected to Easter Island's stone sculpture, yet our recent excavations revealed a treasure trove of rock art superimposed on the statues.

During one of my pre-dissertation forays on Easter Island, Clem wrote me a letter from his UCLA Field School on San Clemente Island. The letter was dated July 4, 1983, and headed "from my island to yours." His colorful description gave me a glimpse of "a very rich site" as well as his sense of fun.

> We are very popular with the Navy, since I brought 15 good-looking girls out to this base and we do not lack for social invitations. Last night we all celebrated the eve of the Fourth by watching a demonstration given by the Navy underwater demolition team . . . It was a blast, literally and figuratively.

He ended with, "I look forward to seeing you return with your Ph.D. thesis in hand, ready for final typing."

Before Clem retired from UCLA, he ensured the Archive's future by putting in place a modest endowment generously provided by then-Archivist Helen Michaelis. His last official effort on behalf of the Archive was to conspire with Tim Earle, then director of the Institute, to rope me into taking the position of Archive director while teaching his UCLA Extension rock art classes.

The year Clem died, the Archive sponsored a symposium on the rock art of Baja California. Clem was slated to participate but, of course, he couldn't, and Billy Clewlow graciously took his place. A cadre of Mexican archaeologists and rock art recorders helped us live up to Clem's dictum of placing rock art in archaeological context. One happy outcome was Harry Crosby's donation to the Archive of his rock art photographs and notes.

Today, the Archive continues a thriving volunteer program and holds 14 named collections, many of which were donated after 1997. The Robert F. Heizer Special Collection, the acquisition of which was facilitated by Clem and Billy Clewlow, maintains Heizer's scholarly narrative and includes the historic and theoretical core of California rock art studies. Our goal is to convert all Archive files to the UC Library System Open Access program. In this, as in all of our efforts, we enjoy the support of the Cotsen Institute of Archaeology and adhere to Clem's dictum that the past, and its history, belongs equally to all of us.

Jo Anne Van Tilburg, Director, Rock Art Archive
The Cotsen Institute of Archaeology, UCLA

His Ideas, Programs, and Personal Influence Shaped a Great Many Lives and Careers   As a long-time admirer of the many significant professional contributions made by the late Professor Clement W. Meighan to the discipline of archaeology and particularly to the research field of California archaeology, I also have retained an enormous appreciation of the influence he had in shaping my own professional life and the lives of a great many of our colleagues.

Clem Meighan first began to influence my own academic direction in the spring semester of 1961, when I took an undergraduate course in world prehistory during my freshman year at UCLA in order to satisfy a general education requirement, and Clem happened to be the instructor. At that time, I was a major in political science, and had never thought of pursuing an education in archaeology. When I was in high school in Dallas, Texas, I had not planned to attend UCLA. I had been accepted at the University of Texas. But halfway through my senior year in high school, my father accepted a job in Los Angeles, and my family planned to move there as soon as I graduated from high school. Thus I applied to UCLA, and in my application I was required to identify a discipline in which I would major. Based on my high school experience, I chose political science. When I took the world prehistory course taught by Clem, however, I became quite mesmerized by the subject of archaeology. I asked for an appointment with him to discuss how I could pursue an undergraduate focus on archaeology.

Clem advised me that I would need to major in anthropology. Since he was department chair at the time, he had no trouble in helping me change my major. He then arranged for me to get training and research experience, which included spring and summer archaeological field schools, and an upper division course he taught in laboratory research methods. It was in that lab class that I met Kerry Kona, who became my wife, another element of Clem's contributions that lives in my heart.

He also had led in the establishment of UCLA's Archaeological Survey, an on-campus institution that provided early days CRM services for government agencies, and therefore also brought in research contracts which helped support students and programs. It mainly was operated by graduate and undergraduate students, giving them exceptional experiences in conducting research in the field and the lab, writing grant proposals and research reports, and managing projects with staffs and budgets. By the time I was a senior, I already had gained the opportunity to direct several small research projects.

Clem provided even richer experiences for his graduate students, including administrative opportunities as leaders of the Archaeological Survey. He provided experiences in publication by establishing the Survey's yearly journal, the *Archaeological Survey Annual Report*, which not only included student-authored papers, but was edited and published by Archaeological Survey administrators, who also were graduate students. His graduate students were also led to cultivate productive relationships with state and federal personnel in programs that managed archaeological resources, which opened up many career directions. These contacts gave graduate students access to more research and grant opportunities and postgraduate careers. Clem's ideas, programs, and personal influence shaped a great many lives and careers in ways that have been very productive for both the individuals and the discipline. Rich memories of his influence continue to live on, with great appreciation.

Joseph L. Chartkoff
Professor Emeritus of Anthropology
Michigan State University, East Lansing, Michigan

A Very Special Person   On September 14, 1953, I walked into Dr. Meighan's office in the basement of Franz Hall for my first interview as a 17-year-old incoming anthropology freshman at UCLA. This short counseling session was the beginning that changed my life both professionally and personally forever. Dr. Meighan was my mentor and friend for over 40 years. He was an inspiring professor, blessed with an uplifting personality, and was particularly animated and fun-loving on field projects.

While he always made field research entertaining, he was also a serious, accomplished archaeologist. During excavations, he sometimes showed an uncanny ability to recognize a possibility the rest of the crew missed. At Paragonah, Utah, the excavation of a subfloor burial exposed a chunk of clay that contained several small holes. Dr. Meighan, realizing their potential significance, had the holes filled with plaster. It turned out that the plaster casts represented wooden prayer sticks with feathers attached!

Thinking back, I especially admire him for providing so many research and employment opportunities to his students. He arranged for one undergraduate student (now my wife) to study pollen analysis at a university in the Southwest. He sent Fred Reinman and me to Catalina Island to disassemble the gross exhibits of human remains at the Glidden Museum. David Pendergast and I were dispatched to the Arizona Strip to salvage the prehistory of the heavily vandalized Antelope Cave. At UCLA, I held positions as museum technician, archaeologist in charge of the Archaeological Survey, archaeological field class instructor, and director of a UCLA Summer Archaeology Field School in Cedar City, Utah. These are just a tiny sample of the hundreds of ways Dr. Meighan helped his students over the years.

Publication was of great importance to Dr. Meighan and he urged students to follow his example by completing at least one article a year. He initiated the *UCLA Archaeological Survey Annual Report* in part to provide them with a publication source. In addition, he co-authored articles and monographs with many of them and, when necessary, found ways to facilitate acceptance of their research in professional journals. Early in my graduate career, he was asked to write a review of *The Topanga Culture* by Treganza and Bierman for *American Antiquity*. He told me

I was an expert on the Topanga Culture and asked me to write the review instead of him. I complied. Years later, after I had accepted a teaching position at Chico State, my monograph on a Topanga site submitted to the UC Press was initially rejected without comment by Robert Heizer. Somehow Dr. Meighan managed to get around him and resolved a few other issues so that the monograph was accepted by the UC Press and published in the *Anthropological Records* series.

Perhaps some measure of Dr. Meighan's professional accomplishments is reflected in the successes of his many students. For example, of those archaeologists who work in California, nine of his students have received the SCA's Lifetime Achievement Award—beginning with Emma Lou Davis in 1982—and still counting.

Regardless of the measurement used, Dr. Meighan was outstanding. He was a very special person!

Keith L Johnson
Professor Emeritus of Anthropology
CSU, Chico

Clem Beyond California   Clem Meighan's career in and contributions to California archaeology are widely recognized, and require little repetition here. Perhaps less well-remembered today are the geographical range of his research and the breadth of his topical and analytical concerns. As one of his many students, I was as much influenced by Clem's catholic interests as by his California research. In an age of increasingly narrow and specialized focus, his career was anything but that, and he readily facilitated those of us who shared a wider archaeological perspective. California prehistory was the foundation of his (and many of his students') careers, but it was also a springboard to other regions and topics. These warrant mention, if only to remind the archaeological world of the depth of his achievements and the wide range of his influence.

Clem's early and groundbreaking work on Catalina Island, with its emphasis on what was then called cultural ecology, was an essential precursor to current debates about the evolution and adaptation of coastal populations. But equally important, and much less appreciated in California, was his overseas research, conducted at about the same time. This started with his west Mexico project, directed with Henry Nicholson from 1956 to 1970 that involved a series of major excavations, and created the first cohort of west Mexican archaeological researchers. It also resulted in his introduction of obsidian hydration dating to two regions where it subsequently has become standard practice: California and Mesoamerica. Obsidian hydration dating labs are now common, throughout the Americas at least. But it was effectively Clem who first brought the technique to archaeology and promoted it as an essential chronometric tool.

While Clem's foundational work in west Mexico, as well as his contributions to the development of obsidian dating, should constitute a major career legacy for any archaeologist, his research ultimately extended much further and had a wider impact. It included excavations and rock art studies in Baja California and Costa Rica, along with projects in the Atacama Desert, Chile, and even in Okinawa—all of which resulted in reports that, like his west Mexican research, have provided the bedrock upon which subsequent regional studies have been based. Clem may not have been the founding father of California archaeology—perhaps this title should go to Bob Heizer, who preceded Clem by a few years—but he was certainly the founding father of archaeological research in a number of other regions of the world.

The emphasis of Clem's work on culture history, ecological adaptation, dating, and rock art is, again, well-known by California archaeologists, because of their relevance to our archaeological record. Perhaps less appreciated is the ethnographic side of his career. This included his emphasis on ethnography as an essential part of any archaeological education, as well as his service on the graduate committees of a variety of cultural anthropological students. Certainly the best known of these was Carlos Castaneda, whose UCLA dissertation (and subsequent books) ultimately became quite controversial. Right or wrong, Carlos was intellectually intense, very private, and extremely hard-working. Clem's favorite comment about Carlos was the fact that, as an undergraduate, he turned in a completed book manuscript to Clem to review—the only undergraduate who, in Clem's long career, had ever done such a thing. This manuscript subsequently became Carlos' M.A. thesis, and *New York Times* best-seller, *Don Juan: A Yaqui Way of Knowledge.*

I mention Carlos for a reason, because it highlights an aspect of Clem's ethnographic career that is likely not appreciated by California archaeologists. This was Clem's contribution to what is currently being described, by historians of ethnography, as the "UCLA school of shamanism." Shamanism was a focus of substantial research at UCLA during the 1960s and 1970s, in large measure due to the influence of Johannes Wilbert and Gerardo Reichel-Dolmatoff. In addition to Carlos, this "school" produced a number of researchers, including Peter Furst, Barbara Meyerhoff, David Joralemon, and Douglas Sharon. (I believe Stacey Shaeffer and I have been designated the last students of this "school.") And while the emphasis of the research was certainly ethnology, it always maintained an archaeological side, perhaps best expressed by Furst's and my own research on prehistoric shamanism. It was largely Clem's influence that promoted this archaeological perspective, and kept prehistory in the discussions of New World shamanism.

Because of the geographical range and topical variability of Clem's research, it is easy to overlook the true significance of his contributions. Certainly there is value in specialization (be it regional, theoretical, or analytical). But I will always be grateful for his encouragement, by word and example, to look beyond California archaeology alone. This ultimately caused me to conduct research across western North America, as well as in Mesoamerica, southern Africa, and the European Upper Paleolithic—and I believe I am a much better archaeologist for that fact. Without Clem's support, I might not have recognized the great importance of this wider archaeological world-view.

David S. Whitley, ASM Affiliates, Inc.
Tehachapi, California

Please submit items for News and Notes to Shelly Davis-King at shellydk@frontiernet.net.

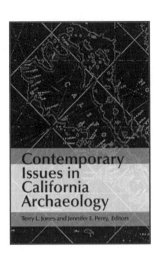